Contents

KT-460-826

AQA introduction		v
Introduction to this book		1

Unit 1 — **Practical problem solving in the digital world** — **2**

Introduction		2
Section 1	**Input**	**4**
	1.1 Input, input devices and media	4
	1.2 Choosing an input device	13
Section 2	**Output**	**15**
	2.1 Output, output devices and media	15
	2.2 Choosing an output device	21
Section 3	**Storage**	**25**
	3.1 Storage devices and media	25
	3.2 Choosing a storage device	28
Section 4	**Software**	**32**
	4.1 Systems software	32
	4.2 Applications software	33
	4.3 Choosing applications software	45
Section 5	**Health and safety**	**49**
	5.1 Health and safety of ICT systems	49
	5.2 Health and safety of software	53
Section 6	**Analysis and design**	**56**
	6.1 Analysis of problems	56
	6.2 Design of solutions	62
Section 7	**Implementation and testing**	**71**
	7.1 Planning for implementation	71
	7.2 Test planning	74
Section 8	**Evaluation**	**81**
	8.1 Assessement of the effectiveness of solutions	81
Examination-style questions		**89**

Unit 2 — **Living in the digital world** — **92**

Introduction		92

Section 9	ICT systems and their components	94
	9.1 What is ICT?	94
	9.2 What is a system?	94
	9.3 What is an ICT system?	95
	9.4 Components of ICT systems	97

Section 10	Data and information	101
	10.1 Data and information	102
	10.2 Coding and encoding	102
	10.3 Processing data	105
	10.4 Quality of information	105

Section 11	People and ICT systems	108
	11.1 ICT systems: design and purpose	108
	11.2 Characteristics of users	108
	11.3 How users interact with ICT systems	111
	11.4 Working in ICT	116

Section 12	Transfer of data in ICT systems	120
	12.1 What is an ICT network?	120
	12.2 Characteristics of a network	121
	12.3 Use of communication technologies	126
	12.4 Standards	127

Section 13	Safety and security of ICT systems	129
	13.1 The need to protect data in ICT systems	129
	13.2 Threats to ICT systems	131
	13.3 How are ICT systems protected?	134
	13.4 Legislation to protect ICT systems	136

Section 14	Procedures for backup and recovery	142
	14.1 Backup	142
	14.2 Recovery	148

Section 15	Uses of ICT systems	153
	15.1 What ICT can provide	153
	15.2 Is the use of ICT systems always appropriate?	157
	15.3 Types of processing	159

Section 16	Factors and consequences of ICT	162
	16.1 Factors influencing the use of ICT systems	162
	16.2 Consequences of the use of ICT	167

Examination-style questions	174

Index	179

Exclusively endorsed by AQA

Stuart McNee
Diane Spencer

Series editor
Claire Rees

Nelson Thornes

EG39544

Text © Stuart McNee and Diane Spencer 2008
Original illustrations © Nelson Thornes Ltd 2008

The right of Stuart McNee and Diane Spencer to be identified as authors of this work has been asserted by them in accordance with the Copyright, Designs and Patents Act 1988.

All rights reserved. No part of this publication may be reproduced or transmitted in any form or by any means, electronic or mechanical, including photocopy, recording or any information storage and retrieval system, without permission in writing from the publisher or under licence from the Copyright Licensing Agency Limited, of Saffron House, 6–10 Kirby Street, London, EC1N 8TS.

Any person who commits any unauthorised act in relation to this publication may be liable to criminal prosecution and civil claims for damages.

Published in 2008 by:
Nelson Thornes Ltd
Delta Place
27 Bath Road
CHELTENHAM
GL53 7TH
United Kingdom

09 10 11 12 / 10 9 8 7 6 5 4 3

A catalogue record for this book is available from the British Library

ISBN 978 0 7487 9907 7

Cover photograph: Alamy/Blend Images
Illustrations by Fakenham Photosetting Ltd
Page make-up by Fakenham Photosetting Ltd

Printed and bound in China by 1010 Printing International Ltd

EG39544
ood MCN
1 wk Main
EHWLC
LEARNING CENTRE EALING GREEN

The authors and publisher are grateful to the following for permission to reproduce photographs and other copyright material in this book:

Fig. 1.1 Lawrence Manning/Corbis; Fig. 1.2a Bellemedia/Fotolia; Fig. 1.2b Peter Ivanov/Fotolia; Fig. 1.3 Martyn F. Chillmaid/Science Photo Library; Fig. 1.4 Xalanx/Fotolia; Fig. 1.6 Charles Stirling/Alamy; Fig. 1.8 Linda & Colin McKie/iStockphoto; Fig. 1.9 Photofusion Picture Library/Alamy; Fig. 1.11 Rex Features; Fig. 2.1a Paddler/Fotolia; Fig. 2.1b Cristimatei/Fotolia; Fig. 2.2 Benoit David/iStockphoto; Fig. 2.3 Photodisc/Alamy; Fig. 2.4 Diego Cervo/Fotolia; Fig. 2.5 Ann Johansson/Corbis; Fig. 4.6 Tom Curtis/Fotolia; Fig. 4.8 http://audacity.sourceforge.net licensed under a Creative Commons License; Fig. 4.9 Sibelius 5 student – Year 9 coursework by permission of Sibelius Software - A Part of Avid; Fig. 9.2 DVLA; Fig. 9.5 Mobiqua; Fig. 10.6 Rick Campbell/iStockphoto; Fig. 11.2 www.8dim.com/products/media-center-interface.asp; Fig. 11.3 www.theage.com.au; Fig. 11.4 Apimac holographic user interface licensed under a Creative Commons License; Fig. 11.5 © 2006 Ted Goranson www.atpm.com; Fig. 11.6 www.biocrawler.com licensed under a Creative Commons License; Fig. 11.7 Microsoft product screen shot(s) reprinted with permission from Microsoft Corporation; Fig. 11.9 Microsoft product screen shots reprinted with permission from Microsoft Corporation; Fig. 11.10 Channel 4 Science Essentials website www.channel4learning.com © Espresso Education Ltd; Fig. 14.4 Roger Ressmeyer/Corbis; Fig. 15.1 Konstantin Sutyagini/Stockphoto; Fig. 15.3 SoDa quoted material from www.soda-is.com; Fig. 15.4 www.earthcam.com/uk/scotland/edinburgh courtesy of EarthCam Inc.; Fig. 15.5 www.odeon.co.uk; Fig. 16.4 Fotolia; Fig. 16.5 www.laptop.org available under Creative Commons Attribution 2.5; Fig. 16.6 www.direct.gov.uk Crown copyright reprinted under Crown copyright PSI License C2008000256.

p101 John Naisbett, *Megatrends*, Warner Books, 1992; p124 'Interconnected digital home' from *PC Plus* May 2006; p150 case studies of Fulcrum Pharma and Wildfowl and Wetlands Trust from *Computing* 2 November 2006 by John Malachy; p156 SoDa quoted material from www.soda-is.com; p168 British Airways case study from *Computing* 19 July 2007.

AQA introduction

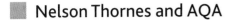

Nelson Thornes and AQA

Nelson Thornes has worked in collaboration with AQA to ensure that this book offers you the best support for your AS Level course and helps you to prepare for your exams. The partnership means that you can be confident that the range of learning, teaching and assessment practice materials has been checked by the senior examining team at AQA before formal approval, and is closely matched to the requirements of your specification.

Blended learning

Printed and electronic resources are blended. This means that links between the topics and activities between the book and the electronic resources, help you to work in the way that best suits you, and enable extra support to be provided online. For example, you can test yourself online and use the feedback from the test to revisit chapter material that may need further work.

Electronic resources are available in a simple-to-use online platform called Nelson Thornes *learning space*. If your school or college has a licence to use the service, you will be given a password with which you can access the materials through any internet connection.

Icons in this book indicate where there is material online related to that topic. The following icons are used:

Learning activity

These resources include a variety of interactive and non-interactive activities to support your learning:

- animations
- presentations
- simple interactive activities
- worksheet activities
- glossary.

Progress tracking

These resources include a variety of tests that you can use to check your knowledge on particular topics (Test yourself) and a range of resources that enable you to analyse and understand examination questions (On your marks...).

Research support

These resources include WebQuests, in which you are assigned a task and provided with a range of web links to use as source material for research. These are designed as Extension resources to stretch you and broaden your learning, in order for you to attain the highest possible marks in your exams.

Study skills

These resources are designed to help students develop skills that are key to this course, for example, in identifying ICT problems and solutions. These resources include data sets, worksheets, sample documents, audio interviews and discussion tools.

Weblinks

Our online resources feature a list of recommended weblinks, split by chapter. This will give you a head start, helping you to navigate to the best websites that will aid your learning and understanding of the topics in your course.

Practical

This icon identifies where there is a relevant practical activity to be undertaken on a computer. Where indicated, support is provided online.

When you see an icon, go to Nelson Thornes *learning space* at www.nelsonthornes.com/aqagce, enter your access details and select your course. The materials are arranged in the same order as the topics in the book, so you can easily find the resources you need.

How to use this book

This book covers the specification for your course and is arranged in a sequence approved by AQA. The main text of the book will cover Units 1 and 2 of the AQA AS Level ICT specification. These units each account for 50% of the overall AS Level mark, or 25% of the full A Level in ICT.

Unit 1 covers problem solving and offers a practical approach to learning and understanding the development of ICT systems. In this unit, you will develop an understanding of the factors that need to be considered when choosing software, hardware and implementing ICT solutions. Although there is no coursework for the AS course, chapters 6 to 8 will aid students in developing the problem solving skills that they would later build on in unit 4 of the A2 course.

Unit 2 develops an understanding of what it is like to live in our technologically-focused age. This unit looks at how ICT systems work and what effect they have on the way we live. It also looks more closely at how this continually evolving process affects ICT professionals, and the qualities that they must have to keep pace and be successful within it.

Unit openers give you a summary of the content you will be covering and give a brief context for each topic/section.

The features in this book include:

Learning objectives

At the beginning of each section you will find a list of learning objectives that contain targets linked to the requirements of the specification. The relevant specification reference is also provided.

Key terms

Terms that you will need to be able to define and understand are highlighted in bold blue type within the text, e.g. **Bluetooth**. You can look up these terms in the glossary online.

PC activities

PC-based activities that will support you in developing skills which are key to the course.

Case studies

Real-life examples to illustrate a point.

Did you know?

Interesting facts to bring learning to life.

Remember

Key points and common errors.

Activities

Suggestions for practical investigations you can carry out.

End-of-topic questions

Short questions that test your understanding of the subject and allow you to apply the knowledge and skills you have acquired to different scenarios.

AQA Examiner's tip

Hints from AQA examiners to help you with your studies and to prepare you for your exam.

AQA Examination-style questions

Questions in the style that you can expect in your exam. These occur at the end of each unit to give practice in examination-style questions for a particular section.

AQA examination questions are reproduced by permission of the Assessment and Qualifications Alliance.

Nelson Thornes is responsible for the solution(s) given and they may not constitute the only possible solution(s).

■ Web links for this book

All websites that are integral to this book can be found at www.nelsonthornes.com/aqaqce/ict_resource.htm

Nelson Thornes is not responsible for third party content online, there may be some changes to this material that are beyond our control. In order for us to ensure that the links referred to are as up-to-date and stable as possible, please let us know at **webadmin@ nelsonthornes.com** if you find a link that doesn't work and we will do our best redirect these, or to list an alternative site.

Introduction to this book

ICT AS Level – the new AQA specification

This exciting new specification has been designed to meet the needs of students studying ICT in the 21st century. Today's students are digital natives, and their expectation of an A level in ICT is one that will motivate, challenge and excite them; this course aims to do precisely that by encouraging students to become active investigators with a full understanding of when, why and how to use ICT appropriately, fully equipping them for a world beyond their A level study.

Unit 1: INFO1 Practical Problem Solving in the Digital World will develop students' knowledge and understanding of ICT systems through practical experience. It offers the opportunity to be truly creative and students should be encouraged to explore the range of ICT options available to them in order to fully develop their skills as the use of current and relevant software, hardware and communication technologies will inspire and enhance their practical work.

Within this unit, students will examine the analysis, design, implementation, testing and evaluation of ICT-related solutions and be made aware of the health and safety issues relating to the use of ICT systems. Through a growing understanding of the available software and hardware for these systems, students are encouraged to critically consider their application, questioning whether the tools they have used are the most appropriate for their purpose. This book and the online materials include activities that help students to develop the logical and analytical skills that they will need to achieve this.

Unit 2: INFO2 Living in the Digital World will develop students' understanding of the wider picture with regard to the use of ICT. The unit aims to embed and extend knowledge of ICT terms and concepts, enabling students to confidently explore the broader issues and consequences relating to the use of ICT in our world. This book, and the accompanying online materials, provide case study examples and a range of bespoke resources, to enable students to fully explore these concepts.

Throughout the development of this new specification, representatives from both industry and higher education were consulted in a continuous effort to ensure that the students following this course would be equipped for their life beyond A levels. They have identified that whilst the knowledge gained through the study of ICT is critical, the successful candidates will need to demonstrate more than a theoretical understanding of ICT to be successful. The real world will involve working in a variety of ways with other people, so it is essential that opportunities are sought for all students to develop the skills of cooperative working that are high on the agenda of companies looking for future employees. The philosophy behind this specification is supported by industry, which seeks employees who understand both ICT *and* business; a representative from industry said of the new specification, 'I would actually employ students who had completed this course.'

This new specification, building on the strengths of the existing one, brings the study of ICT into the 21st century and provides students with the skills required by real ICT professionals.

Practical problem solving in the digital world

Sections in this unit:

1 Input

2 Output

3 Storage

4 Software

5 Health and safety

6 Analysis and design

7 Implementation and testing

8 Evaluation

Introduction

This unit provides the opportunity for candidates to develop their knowledge and understanding of the development of ICT systems through practical experience of using a range of applications software in a structured way, to create solutions to realistic problems for clients, end users and their audiences.

Students will need to take evidence of work generated through this module into the examination and be prepared to discuss their methodologies and results. These transferable skills can then be applied to unfamiliar situations within an examination.

Within this unit you will learn to identify and analyse a problem in order to define input, output and processing requirements. This will provide the necessary firm foundation for designing an appropriate ICT solution.

The design of effective solutions needs to consider all aspects of the solution. Data entry methods and validation techniques, together with other methods of maintaining data integrity need to be designed carefully. Processing functions need to be effective and efficient, leading to a robust, workable solution that produces relevant, useable output matching to the needs of the client. Furthermore the designs need to be documented in such a way that they could be used by others to re-create the solution.

The effectiveness of the solution needs to be tested realistically, systematically and thoroughly, with appropriate data sets and testing methodologies used to provide evidence of the strengths and weaknesses of the solution. Normal, extreme and erroneous data all have their role in this testing process.

Evaluating the effectiveness of solutions involves reviewing the client specification and assessing the extent to which the solution fulfils its requirements. Improvements and enhancements will suggest strategies that could be applied to future project work and the evaluation exercise provides a sound foundation for A2 study.

Specification	Topic content	Page
Selection and use of input devices and media	Input, input devices and media Choosing an input device	4 13
Selection and use of output devices and media	Output, output devices and media Choosing an output device	15 21
Selection and use of storage devices and media	Storage devices and media Choosing a storage device	25 28
Selection and use of appropriate software	Systems software Applications software Choosing applications software	32 33 45
Health and safety in relation to the use of ICT systems	Health and safety of ICT systems Health and safety of software	49 53
Analysis and design of solutions	Analysis of problems Design of solutions	56 62
Implementation & testing of ICT solutions	Planning for implementation Testing planning	71 74
Evaluation of ICT-related solutions	Assessment of the effectiveness of solutions	81

1 Input

In this section you will cover:

- what forms data input to a computer can take

- what input devices are available and what media they use

- how to choose an input method when designing a solution to a problem.

AQA Examiner's tip

Be very careful not to confuse the words data and information when answering a question about input devices. In everyday language, people talk about entering information, but in ICT it is important to be accurate and write about entering data.

Remember

It is important not to confuse inputs and input devices. If you enter clients' names using a keyboard, the **input data** are the names, the **data type** is text and the **input device** is the keyboard. If you feed something into the input device, such as a multiple choice examination paper, the paper is the **media**.

Data types

Section 10 of this book covers data more fully than this one, but it is impossible to think about input devices without thinking of data. The main data types that can be put into a computer system are:

- text
- still and moving images
- numbers
- sound.

1.1 Input, input devices and media

Input devices

Manual input

Most computer systems come with a keyboard and mouse as standard.

Keyboard

The most common input device in most computer systems is the standard QWERTY keyboard. This will have keys for all the letters and numbers plus special keys such as ESC, ALT, CTRL, SHIFT and the function keys. There are variations on this layout in different countries, and some keyboards will have extra keys such as a numeric keypad. Ergonomic keyboards have been designed to try to reduce repetitive strain injury (RSI), but people used to the standard keyboard may be reluctant to change to one of a different shape.

Fig. 1.1 *Ergonomic keyboard*

Devices like mobile phones also use smaller versions of keyboards, which are usually called keypads. They often use multiple key presses to select letters, as a full-sized keyboard would clearly not be practical in devices of this size.

Mouse

The mouse is still the most common pointing device used to move a pointer around the screen and to select options by clicking. A mouse can be connected to the computer via a cable or wirelessly.

There are two main types of mouse, mechanical and optical. A mechanical mouse has a rolling ball and the computer senses its position on a flat surface. They work best on a mouse mat.

An optical mouse uses a light sensor to detect motion and does not need a mouse mat.

Both types of mouse will usually have two or three buttons that can be clicked and many have a scroll wheel to make dragging and scrolling easier.

A trackball does the same job as a mouse, but it has a ball on the surface rather than underneath. The ball is rolled using the fingers or the palm of the hand. They are sometimes used with laptop computers because they are easier to use in confined spaces.

Many laptops have trackpads, where the user moves their finger over a sensitive plate to control the cursor.

A trackpoint is a small button that works like a joystick and is sometimes seen on mobile phones, PDAs and laptops.

Fig. 1.2 *Trackpads and trackpoints can be used to control cursor movement on laptops*

Touch-sensitive devices

These devices, as their name suggests, respond to touch for data input.

Concept keyboards

A concept keyboard is divided into areas which are labelled to suit the actual use. Special software then interprets the key press for the computer. They can be used in checkout tills or restaurants, so that the user can press the name of the item sold rather than having to remember the price of it. The keyboard may have a plastic film over it to protect it from food and drink spills.

Concept keyboards are also used as input devices for children or for people with disabilities. A small child might hear a question asking what colour an object is. They respond by pressing the correct section of a keyboard that has been divided into six sections, each representing a colour.

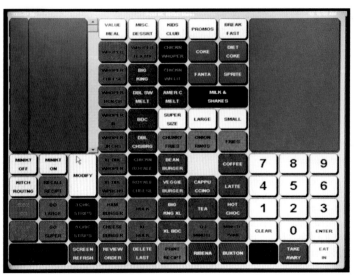

Fig. 1.3 *A point-of-sale touchscreen display*

Touch screens

A touch screen senses when an area of the screen has been touched, either by wires embedded in the screen or by patterns of infra-red light beams. Software then interprets the signal.

Touch screens are often used in public areas because they are easy to use, combine input and output and don't need any extra devices such as a mouse. They usually allow a limited selection of items from a menu, but can have a virtual keyboard for short items of text.

PDAs often use touch screens as combined input/output devices. A small **stylus**, or even a fingertip, is used to select items, draw or write. They often have handwriting recognition software so that handwritten notes can be converted into characters that can be processed by the computer. The software compares the characters drawn with a dictionary of letters and numbers. It may need to be 'trained' to recognise the handwriting of the person using it.

Key terms

PDA: a personal digital assistant is a small computer, about the size of a hand, so sometimes called a palmtop.

Stylus: a small stick used to select or draw on a touch screen.

Fig. 1.4 *PDA with stylus*

Activity

Using the Internet look for the latest PDA and mobile phone devices. Make a list of the forms of input they accept.

Graphics tablets

Graphics tablets (sometimes called digitising tablets) are used mainly for drawing. A stylus is used to draw on a flat plate. The stylus feels rather like a pencil, and so is more natural to draw with than a mouse. It can also be used to select icons or for writing in languages such as Chinese that use drawn characters rather than letters. Many users find them easier to use than a Chinese keyboard.

Interactive whiteboards are touch-sensitive computer displays, often used in schools. The teacher can draw on the screen with a stylus shaped like a pen, and many boards allow things to be moved around the screen using fingers. The image is projected on to the screen, and so the boards are combined input and output devices.

Speech recognition

Speech recognition involves the user speaking into a microphone. The sounds of the words are compared with a dictionary of sounds and converted into computer-readable text using speech recognition software. Speech recognition is still not very reliable, because different voices and accents can make the same word sound very different. The system has to be trained to match certain patterns with certain words for specific users. The process is also complicated by words that sound the same but are spelled differently, such as 'there' and 'their', although sophisticated software tries to overcome this by looking at the context of the word before choosing a match. The results are likely to be better if each word is spoken separately and distinctly, but this does slow down the process.

Did you know?

Digital signatures

Touch screen signature pads are used to add signatures to electronic documents. Many parcel delivery services use them to obtain signatures from customers on delivery. The customer uses a stylus on a portable device carried by the delivery driver.

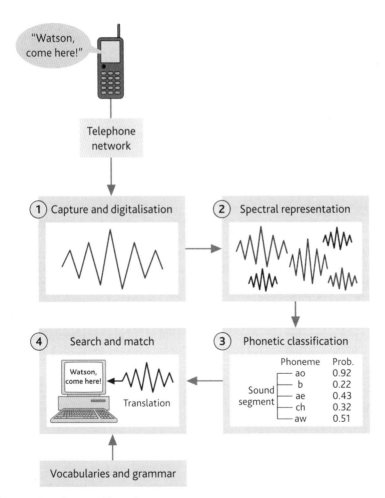

Fig. 1.5 *Speech recognition software*

Automated input

Some input devices read data from media that have the data stored on them. Sometimes the data is stored magnetically, sometimes on paper-based media that are scanned and interpreted by software.

■ **Did you know?**

Some banks are planning to issue pre-paid cards that are suitable for buying small value items. An amount of money would be 'loaded' onto the card, so that when the customer bought a low-price item such as a newspaper, the card would be read and the total amount of money left would be reduced. The retailer would not have to pay a high charge and people would not have to worry so much about getting cash to pay for things. The card would then be 'topped up' as and when necessary.

■ **Key terms**

Radio frequency ID (RFID): a way of tracking objects by attaching a transmitter that sends a signal giving the serial number and its location.

Fig. 1.6 *RFID transmitters are used in Oyster cards, 'smartcards' used for travelling around London on public transport.*

Card readers

Plastic or paper cards can be used to store data in various ways:

■ Magnetic strip cards are swiped through a card reader or fed into a slot in the card reader machine. They are easy to read, but can't hold very much data. The magnetic strip is also quite easy to scratch.

■ A smart card, such as a chip-and-PIN credit card, has a computer chip built into it that can hold far more data than a strip card, and can also have data written to it. The use of the card has to be authorised by a personal identification number (PIN), making it more secure than a swipe card authorised by a signature. The chip also means that the data can be encrypted, which improves security. Cards with chips can have data loaded that can be changed each time the card is used; so for example a £20 gift card can be bought in a store, and each time the person uses it, the amount spent is deducted from the total money available.

Radio frequency ID

Radio frequency identification (RFID) uses radio waves to transmit a unique serial number as a form of ID for objects. A tag is attached to an object or to a box or pallet, and the tag transmits the serial number to a reader which sends the data on to a computer. Software is used to track the position of the item. RFID tags are sometimes called smart labels or radio bar codes.

At the moment the biggest use of RFID is in transport and logistics, as companies can trace goods through the supply chain from the manufacturer to the point of sale. They can also be used by hospitals to locate expensive equipment quickly to improve patient care.

■ **Activity**

RFID tags can be fitted to most items we buy. If the tags are not removed or deactivated, they can still be tracked by the reader. Some people think this is a potential invasion of privacy. Use the Internet or other sources to research varying opinions on RFID. Discuss whether or not you think the potential benefits outweigh the drawbacks and what safeguards, if any, you think should be in place to protect consumers.

www.rfid.com is the website of the Independent European Centre for RFID. The BBC news site has many articles expressing opinions about their use.

Scanners

Scanners are used to turn paper-based pictures or documents into digital images. A beam of light passes across the page and senses the colour of various areas. There are various types of scanner:

■ Flat-bed scanners have a flat glass plate on to which the document is placed.

■ Bar code scanners in supermarkets are a form of flat-bed scanner.

■ Hand-held scanners are mainly used in shops that sell large items which cannot be lifted on to a scanning plate.

■ In sheet-feed scanners the scanner head stays still and the paper is moved over it.

■ Drum scanners give very high-definition images.

The quality of the picture being scanned depends on the resolution the scanner has been set to. The higher the resolution, the higher the quality of the picture, but the bigger the file size. Images that are to be displayed on screen can be lower resolution than images to be printed. Resolution is usually measured in dots per inch.

Scanners are also used as the basis of other technologies such as optical mark recognition and optical character recognition.

Optical mark recognition

Used mostly for multiple choice examinations and lottery tickets, **optical mark recognition (OMR)** uses a light beam to sense the position of pencil or other marks on a piece of paper. The software allocates a value to the data depending on where the mark is on the paper. The forms for OMR need to be specially printed, and the software needs to be configured for each one, so this method is fairly expensive to set up, but the results are produced quickly and accurately, so the investment is worthwhile where the volume of data is large. OMR only allows the user to select from a list of choices, so it is a fairly inflexible input method.

Optical character recognition

In **optical character recognition (OCR)**, a paper-based document is scanned and each part of the image is compared to a dictionary of known letter shapes. The letters are then converted into computer characters. Good quality software will also recognise the layout and formatting of the original document. This is easiest if the text was printed from a computer originally.

Many organisations now use OCR technology to input forms that have been filled in by their clients or employees. The forms are divided into boxes, and one upper-case letter is written in each box. The structure of the form and the fact that all the letters are upper case makes it easier for the software to identify each letter. The big disadvantage of this method is that it takes the user a long time to fill in the form, and if they make a mistake, they have to start all over again. This tends to limit its use to forms that people need to fill in, such as passport applications. If businesses adopted this method, many people would not be prepared to spend the extra time on something from which they gain no personal benefit. OCR is much quicker for the organisation than having the data entered manually.

■ **Key terms**

Optical mark recognition (OMR): senses the position of marks on data capture forms such as multiple choice exam papers or lottery entry sheets.

Optical character recognition (OCR): uses a scanner and specialist software to turn paper-based text into computer characters.

The scanner takes a picture of a paper-based document.

OCR software looks at each letter shape and matches it to its dictionary of shapes to convert it to text.

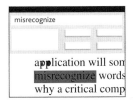

The spell check queries letters that didn't scan clearly or words it doesn't recognise.

An electronic copy of the document is created.

Fig. 1.7 *Paper-based documents can be converted to electronic files by OCR technology*

OCR is more difficult when normal handwriting is involved, as people's handwriting styles vary so much, but a lot of research has been carried out to make it work. Many examination scripts are now scanned and recognised before being sent to markers electronically rather than them being posted. The answer to each question must be written within a box outlined on the paper. The examiners enter marks electronically.

Bar-code readers

A bar code is a pattern of black and white lines which represents a number. They are often used in **electronic point of sale (EPOS)** systems. Most commercial products carry a bar code as part of their packaging. The bar code is scanned, and the product number it generates is entered into the computer system and acts as the primary key for the product in the stock database.

Bar codes have built-in error checking. The final number is a check digit, formed by a calculation using the other digits of the number. If that digit doesn't match, the scanner shows a red light or makes a beeping noise, and the bar code is rejected. The operator will then type in the bar-code number using a key pad. Bar codes are also often used in libraries and other applications where a number needs to be entered into the computer because they save the operator time compared to keying in the data and reduce the chances of a mistake being made as the numbers are keyed.

Magnetic ink character recognition

Magnetic ink character recognition (MICR) is used almost exclusively by banks to process cheques and other negotiable documents. Important numbers such as the cheque number and account number are printed along the bottom of the cheque in uniquely shaped characters using an ink containing magnetic particles. A magnetic reader translates them into numbers that can be stored by the computer system. This technology is used much less now as a greater number of payments are made electronically via credit and debit cards or directly between accounts using online banking. In fact many shops and restaurants no longer accept cheques as a method of payment because, unlike credit and debit card payments, they have no way of checking whether the money is available in the account.

Sound input

When a sound is made and fed into a microphone it creates an analogue signal, like the one shown in Fig. 1.8. The signal is made up of constantly changing voltages.

If this sound is to be entered into a computer, it has to be encoded as a digital signal. To do this, the sound is **sampled**. The voltage is measured many times a second, and a digital equivalent of the waveform is produced. The **sample rate** controls the quality of the sound produced, as the waveform is closer to the original. High sampling rates measure the voltage up to 50,000 times each second, producing good quality sound but large file sizes.

Music can be entered into a computer through instruments linked to the computer via MIDI (Musical Instrument Digital Interface). A digital keyboard has black and white keys like a piano but also has sliders and voice controls to change the sound produced, so that the music can sound as if it is being played by a violin or a flute rather than a keyboard. The instrument can also add background rhythms to support the player. Composers can also play the piece of music several times, each as a

Key terms

Electronic point of sale (EPOS): uses bar codes to enter product numbers at shop tills that are linked to stock databases.

Magnetic ink character recognition (MICR): uses magnetic ink to print characters shaped to ANSI standards which can be read and used to direct cheques and other negotiable documents to their proper financial institutions.

Sampling: a way of recording sound digitally so that it can be input into a computer.

Sample rate: number of times per second a sound reading is taken.

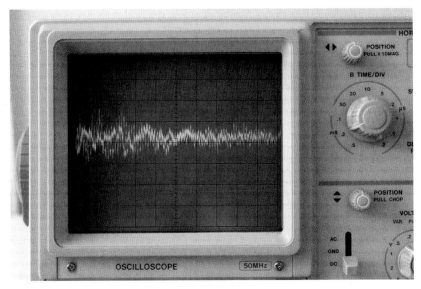

Fig. 1.8 *Sound wave on an oscilloscope*

different instrument, and the sounds can then be mixed to sound as if many people are playing.

Video input

A video picture is made up of many still pictures played very rapidly in sequence to trick the eye into thinking that the movement is continuous. Digital video cameras record the images on to hard disk, DV tape or DVD. The data is later loaded into a computer to be edited. Most digital video cameras can also take still photographs, but their quality is limited because video images do not need to be high resolution.

Many digital cameras and mobile phones are capable of recording fairly short pieces of video.

Webcams

Webcams are small video cameras that are often used for **video conferencing**. They tend not to be particularly high quality, which keeps file size down, and the video images are sent to the computer in a continuous stream. Personal videoconferencing has become much easier through instant messaging and Internet phone services, and so many users have a webcam fixed to their monitor so that they can see their friends as they chat. The Internet also has lots of websites that feature webcams permanently pointed at places of interest, from African watering holes to town centres. The images tend not to be refreshed very often, as this keeps the file size low.

Digital cameras

Digital cameras usually record digital images of the scene being photographed. Budget-model cameras have built-in storage, but most record the images to solid-state digital media such as compact flash or XD cards. The camera can be connected directly to the computer by cable or wirelessly through **Bluetooth**, and the image can be uploaded so that it can be printed or edited. Many cameras also connect directly to printers via Bluetooth, and bypass the computer altogether. Cameras tend to be rated by their maximum resolution, usually quoted in **Megapixels (Mp)**. The camera resolution can be varied, so that images for the Internet can be recorded at low resolution whilst those to be printed can be saved

> ### Key terms
>
> **Video conferencing:** captures and transmits sound and video to allow people in different locations to see and talk to each other.
>
> **Pixel:** a single dot of an image, usually rectangular or square. 1 Megapixel (Mp) is 1 million pixels.
>
> **Bluetooth:** a brand name; it is a method of transmitting data over short distances wirelessly.

at higher resolution. Pictures can be viewed on a built-in screen, and unwanted ones can be deleted to save space. Most mobile phones also have built-in cameras, some with quite a high resolution.

Professional photographers will use digital single lens reflex (DSLR) cameras, which can have extra lenses added to allow them to capture a variety of images – close ups, distant landscapes, etc. The photographer is likely to want to choose the camera settings manually to give total flexibility. Amateur photographers will usually prefer an automatic compact camera with fewer functions because they are easier to carry around and take good pictures without needing a great deal of skill.

Special-purpose input devices

Input devices for people with disabilities

Many standard input devices can be adapted to make them easier for a range of people to use:

Fig. 1.9 *Foot mouse*

- The pointer speed of the mouse can be adjusted to make positioning easier.
- The speed of mouse clicks can be adjusted.
- The buttons on the mouse can be set for left- or right-handed use.
- The numeric keypad can be set to move the pointer in place of a mouse.
- A large trackball may make moving the pointer easier for a user with limited mobility.
- Single keystrokes can be set to replace combined ones like Ctrl Alt Del.
- Concept keyboards can be used to simplify the interface by restricting the number of input options.
- A foot mouse is available that allows the user to control the cursor using foot pedals rather than hands.

Fig. 1.10 *A large trackball can make moving the pointer easier if you have limited mobility*

Games controllers

Computer games often demand fast response times, and many manufacturers make special controllers for them. Some games simulate activities such as driving or flying a plane, and the input device is an important part of making the experience feel real. More advanced versions of these devices are used on professional training simulators.

Wii

Nintendo's Wii remote is used to control their Wii console. It is a one-handed remote control that works by sensing motion and it communicates with the computer via Bluetooth. It can be used left or right handed, and several remotes can be used at once in multi-player games. It can also be used as a pointing device, linking to a sensor bar via infra-red technology. Extra devices have been released to change the Wii into a gun, a sword, a steering wheel or sporting devices such as a golf club or tennis racquet.

1.2 Choosing an input device

There are lots of things to think about when you choose an input device for a particular situation:

- type of data
- volume of data
- user preferences
- cost considerations
- where the device is to be used.

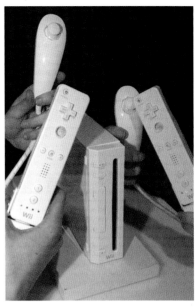

Fig. 1.11 *Multi-function Wii controller*

For example, a dental practice may have lots of data to enter each time a new patient registers. One possibility would be for the patients to enter their own data, perhaps via a web based form or input screens in the surgery. Assuming the data is to be input by staff at the practice from data supplied on paper-based forms, they could:

- enter the data manually using a keyboard plus a mouse for selecting options such as drop-down lists and radio buttons
- redesign the data input form for OCR input
- read the text into a microphone and use voice-recognition software
- write the text on a graphics tablet and use handwriting recognition software.

Using a keyboard and mouse would not involve any extra expense in terms of hardware, but would involve a great deal of operator time. Lots of manual input could cause RSI, so there are possible health and safety implications.

OCR input would involve initial expenditure on hardware and software and redesigned forms. If the forms were filled in carefully, the data should be quicker to input than manual methods. Some patients might find it difficult to fill in a form where they have to write a letter in each box, and it might be enough to make them choose another dentist.

Voice recognition software would need the forms to be read out very slowly, and would be slower than using a skilled data-entry operator. The software would probably also not cope very well with names.

Handwritten text would be impractical for anything other than small amounts of data, and doesn't really have any advantages in this situation.

The practical choice is really either manual input or OCR. OCR would cost more to set up, but would be cost-effective if the volumes of data were large enough. Whether the patients would object or not is another consideration. Patients with disabilities or difficulties with writing clearly might need the form to be filled in for them. OCR is still likely to leave some mistakes in the data because handwriting may not always be clear, and so manual verification would also need to take place.

Activity

A college has a shop selling books and stationery to students. It also has colour and black and white photocopiers for the students to use themselves, where they pay for each copy they make. At the moment the system is completely manual, but the shop is considering moving to a computer-based system. Discuss the input devices that could be used in such a situation, together with their advantages and disadvantages. Include a list of the factors you would need to bear in mind when choosing the best option.

In this, as in many cases, there is no single right answer, but manual input is probably the most practical unless very large amounts of data are involved. A well-designed input form that keeps mouse clicks and keystrokes to a minimum should help to speed up data entry. The screen-based form should also follow a similar layout to the paper-based one.

☑ *In this section you have covered:*

- devices that allow users to enter data manually, such as a keyboard or mouse
- devices that capture sound, such as a microphone
- devices that capture images, such as a digital camera or a digital video camera
- devices that improve accessibility, such as a trackball or foot mouse
- devices that make the input mimic another object such as a pencil, a steering wheel or a sword
- automatic data-capture techniques such as bar codes, optical character recognition and optical mark recognition
- things to think about when choosing an input device – type of data, volume of data, needs of user and cost versus efficiency issues
- limitations of various types of device.

2 Output

In this section you will cover:

- what forms output from a computer can take

- what output devices are available and what media they use

- how to choose an output method when designing a solution to a problem.

> **Remember**
>
> Printed information is often called **hard copy**.

> **Key terms**
>
> **Resolution:** the number of dots that make up an image on screen or on paper.

Information types

Just as data can be of several different types, the information output from a computer can take different forms too. Information can be visual – text or pictures to be viewed on screen or on paper – or it can be audible – sound played through speakers or headphones.

2.1 Output, output devices and media

Output devices

Visual output

- Most computer information is viewed on a monitor as it is created or worked on.

Screens and monitors

Most PC systems are connected to a monitor so that the user can see what is happening as they work or view a finished product such as a document or an animation. Monitors have the advantage of being able to display a moving image rather than just the static ones that can be produced by a printer.

The image quality of a monitor depends on its size and its **resolution**. Most computers allow the user to set the resolution they want to work at. Screens set to high resolution display detailed images, but the images are smaller in size than they would be on a screen set to a lower resolution. Graphic artists and architects work on complex graphics that need large, good quality displays and so they buy large, high-resolution monitors.

The resolution of a monitor display is measured in **pixels**. A laptop monitor might be set to 1280 × 800 pixels, a mobile screen to 320 × 240 pixels.

Fig. 2.1 *CRT and TFT monitors*

> **Remember**
>
> Monitors are sometimes called visual display units, or VDUs.

■ Most monitors are either CRT or TFT types.

CRT monitor

CRT monitors are based on cathode ray tubes that fire electrons at a screen to make each pixel glow in the correct colour. The length of a cathode ray tube means that CRT monitors are deep and take up a lot of room. Many users still use CRT monitors, which give clear, sharp displays at a low cost, but most new systems will be sold with TFT monitors.

TFT monitor

TFT (thin film transistor) monitors are much flatter, and so take up less room than CRT monitors. They use liquid crystals to form the image, and so should really be called TFT LCD monitors. Their small size makes them extremely popular, even though the image on cheaper TFT screens may not be as clear as the equivalent size CRT.

Large displays

If the image produced by a computer needs to be shown to large numbers of people, there are several alternatives.

Digital projectors

Digital projectors can be used to project a large version of the monitor output onto a screen so that it can be viewed by a larger audience in a classroom or for business presentations. They can be portable, but are often ceiling mounted so that they don't need to be set up each time they are used. They vary in brightness (measured in lumens), and brighter projectors are needed for very large rooms or in bright conditions.

Interactive whiteboards

Digital projectors can also be used to project images on to interactive whiteboards. The whiteboards have a touch-sensitive surface that can be 'written on' using a stylus shaped like a marker pen or a finger. They are often used in classrooms to allow students to share their ideas with others, and take part in interactive activities. Handwriting recognition can be used to convert handwritten text to computer text, and the work produced can be saved or printed. Interactive whiteboards are both input and output devices.

Plasma screens

Large plasma screens are often used as TVs, but they can be used instead of normal computer monitors, and are often seen in public areas such as shopping centres and reception areas of businesses. They work by illuminating tiny fluorescent lights to make the image. They are available in very large sizes, and whole banks of them can be used together to make huge wall-mounted displays.

Small displays

Mobile phone screens

An increasing number of mobile phones come with software pre-installed to enable Internet access, and more and more people are using their phone to check e-mail, weather, travel instructions or the football scores. 3G phones can also display live video, so they require a good quality image which refreshes quickly. A 2-inch square TFT mobile phone screen can display 16 million colours at a resolution of 320×240 pixels, making it much more practical to use than older models were. These tiny screens provide real challenges for web designers who need to design webpage content so that it is useable in such a small display area. Many

■ **Did you know?**

A wireless graphics tablet can be used to control the image from anywhere in the room, and can be passed around so that other people in the room can write on the board or carry out interactive activities without leaving their seat.

■ **Did you know?**

Most railway stations have fast ticket systems based on touch screens. They can be used to buy tickets without waiting at the ticket window for an operator, or to collect tickets that have been pre-ordered over the Internet. The screen shows selection menu buttons, and has a virtual keypad so that users can input letters and numbers. The kiosk has a built-in printer that prints tickets and receipts.

TV companies also allow phone users to download content that can be viewed or listened to on mobile devices so that people can, for instance, watch the news on the train as they travel to work.

PDAs

PDAs generally have a larger screen than mobile phones and users expect to be able to run application software such as word processors and spreadsheets on them. This inevitably means that the user has to scroll around to see large documents, but designers try to keep this to a minimum by designing screen layouts carefully. They usually have touch screens so that the overall size can be kept down, and part of the screen is usually devoted to a virtual keyboard that is operated by a stylus.

Printers

Many computer processes need information output in a paper-based format.

💡 Laser printers

Laser printers print a full page at a time in a similar way to a photocopier. The image is formed on the page using a laser beam on a light-sensitive drum that uses electrostatic charges to attract toner particles. The page then passes over a heated fuser unit to melt the toner on to the page.

Monochrome lasers are very popular in offices and other situations where they need high-quality documents printed quickly, and colour is not very important.

Colour laser printers have recently become much less expensive to buy, and so more people are buying them. They use three colours of toner, cyan, magenta and yellow, plus the usual black one. Colour laser printers produce clear text and diagrams, but photographs are likely to be limited in quality compared to high-resolution inkjet printers, as the resolution they use tends to be lower and fewer colours are used.

💡 Inkjet printers

Inkjet printers are very popular, in particular for home use, because they tend to be cheaper to buy than lasers, although they can be expensive to run, and are generally slower than laser printers. The basic models have three ink colours plus black, and they work by spraying ink on to the paper. Photo printers have very high resolution and often many more colours than the basic three, which means they can reproduce the colours in the photograph accurately. When used with coated paper, they can produce photographs close to professional quality. Specialist papers are available that allow prints to be transferred to other items such as clothes, mouse mats or even mugs.

Multi-function printers

Multi-function printers include a built-in scanner, and so can be used as a simple photocopier, suitable for home or small office use. They often have fax facilities too. They usually use inkjet rather than laser technology.

Dot-matrix printers

The main use for dot-matrix technology is to print on **multipart stationery**. Large line printers can print very quickly, use continuous stationery, and are usually used in industrial situations where high-volume prints are needed and quality is not very important. They are used infrequently now as other printing methods have become cheaper and faster than dot-matrix technology. Some cash tills in shops use small

Remember

Portable devices such as PDAs, mobile phones and MP3 players are gradually converging by using more of the same features. You should try to keep up with the latest developments in these devices by reading technology articles in magazines or on websites.

Key terms

Multipart stationery: is made up of several layers, usually in different colours. When they are fed through a dot matrix printer, several copies are printed at once.

17

dot-matrix printers and multipart stationery to produce a copy of the receipt for the customer, whilst retaining a copy for the shop. These use heated wires and heat-sensitive paper to produce text that is of fairly low quality and tends to fade over time.

Plotters

Flat-bed plotters use pens which move across the paper to draw a detailed and accurate image. Other plotters move the paper across rollers whilst the pens move backwards and forwards. They are used mostly to print large-sized technical drawings, although smaller models are available for drawing graphs, and some can be fitted with small blades so that letters and shapes can be cut out of the material on the plotter to make signs or shapes.

Many engineers and architects now use very large inkjet printers rather than plotters for printing out plans and drawings on paper up to A0 size. They are extremely expensive to buy, and are only used for specialist purposes, but they have the advantage of being able to produce full-colour graphics, whereas the pen plotters can only draw lines and shaded areas.

Fig. 2.2 *Plotter*

Professional printers

A small company needing a large amount of the same document may well find it more cost effective to send the files to a professional print shop to be printed. Most towns will have several print shops and there are also lots of companies that offer these services over the Internet. The files can be e-mailed to the print shop and the resulting documents can be posted or collected from a local shop. Most print houses will accept files in Adobe Acrobat format, which has become the standard document viewing format, as anyone can download the software to view such documents.

Professional printers will usually use offset litho printing, which involves making images of each of the colours that are involved and printing them one after the other on top of each other. The documents are printed on to huge rolls of paper, and then cropped to the finished size using powerful cutting tools which leave a very clean edge.

Using a professional printing service saves staff time, produces excellent results, and reduces wear and tear on office printers. It also allows users

Fig. 2.3 *Offset printing press*

to print large documents without having to buy expensive large format printers, whilst still allowing design work to be done in house. Many printers will offer a design service too. The cost per copy reduces with the quantity required, so it is more likely to be economical for large numbers of copies.

Photo printing

Most people with digital cameras like to be able to print their own photos, and buy a printer capable of doing so. There are specialist printers available that only print 6 inch × 4 inch photographs. These are convenient and easy to carry around, and can either be linked directly to the camera via cable or Bluetooth, or print from a memory card taken from the camera. They produce photographs of an acceptable quality, but are expensive to run. Most new inkjet printers can also print photographs, and their quality will vary depending on their resolution and the type of ink used. Photo-quality ink is more expensive than ink suitable for text, and this type of printer can be expensive to run for standard documents.

Another issue with photographs is how long they last. Many people will want to keep photographs permanently as a record of important events, and in this case it is important that the paper and inks used are of archival quality. Not all domestic photo printers can do this. Dye sublimation printers use wax-based inks which can last a long time, and these are gradually becoming available for domestic use.

Professional photo printing can still work out much cheaper than printing at home, and many chemists and supermarkets offer photo developing services from CDs or memory cards, or by linking to the phone or camera via Bluetooth. Many Internet companies offer the same services, plus specialist printing such as photo books, printing on canvas and gift items such as key rings and mugs. Some also offer photo storage facilities.

Most people take far more pictures than they print, and digital photo frames provide a way of displaying photographs without having to print them. They contain screens that display slide shows of photographs stored on a memory card.

Activity

Imagine you are in charge of publicity for your local theatre group, and you need to advertise their new production. You need 10 A0-sized posters, 250 A3-sized posters, 5,000 A5-sized fliers and 5,000 business-card-sized adverts. All of them are single sided, printed in full colour. Using the Internet, or local printing services, compare the cost of producing all these documents. Using the same companies, find the cost of producing half as many of each type. Is it half the original price?

If you have the information available, compare the cost of printing the A5 fliers on facilities you have available to you at school or college.

PC activity

Set up a spreadsheet that will work out the total cost for printing various amounts of the documents mentioned above.

Fig. 2.4 *Bluetooth headset*

Did you know?

If a person has lost the use of one or more senses, it can be quite tiring to have to use the remaining senses all the time. Vibrating alerts like those used on a mobile phone set to silent mode can take the place of either sound or visual outputs, and can sometimes stop one sensory channel from being overloaded. A vibrating alert could be useful for a partially sighted or deaf person to warn them of the arrival of an e-mail.

Speakers

External speakers are plugged into the computer and play sounds and music produced by the sound card. They vary a great deal in size, quality and appearance and in the level of volume they produce.

Many monitors and laptops have built-in speakers that play sound of relatively low quality, suitable for general-purpose use, but not of high enough quality for music or some games players. They are also fairly limited in volume, as they are designed for personal use. Satellite navigation systems also usually have built-in speakers.

Headphones plug into the computer and produce the sound directly into the user's ear, so that other people in the room cannot hear it. This can be useful for MP3 players and in other public situations such as on a bus or train. They are also used in call centres so that each operator can hear their caller whilst keeping the overall level of sound in the room to a minimum. Prolonged use of headphones can cause hearing damage unless the volume is kept low, and some headphones have settings to restrict the maximum volume at which they operate.

Wireless headsets, operating through Bluetooth, can be more convenient than cabled ones, and are often used to make mobile phones hands-free for use in cars.

Special-purpose output devices

Outputs for people with disabilities

A large monitor will make things clearer for partially sighted users. They may need to adjust the display on their monitor by:

- increasing the size of the font
- adjusting the screen resolution
- magnifying the display by zooming in, although this may mean the user has to scroll around a lot
- adjusting the colour contrast between font and background – certain colours are more visible for people with some visual impairments.

Using sound rather than visual output may also be useful:

- text can be read as it is typed, and spell check set to audible rather than visual websites can use key words to describe graphics – the keywords are read out as the page loads.

Braille printers are available that print patterns of raised dots that represent letters and numbers and can be read using the fingers. Reading Braille is not easy, and it is mostly read by people who were born with very little sight rather than people who have lost their sight in later life.

People with little or no hearing can become more independent by using systems that convert sounds, for instance from a telephone call, into sign language using virtual signing systems.

2.2 Choosing an output device

Monitors and screens

There are very few situations where a screen of some kind is not going to be needed, and the main issues when deciding which one to use are size and resolution.

What kind of image needs to be viewed?

A graphics designer, web designer or architect is likely to need to view and work on large, extremely detailed images. A large monitor may take up extra desk space, but will reduce the need to scroll to see all of the image. The monitor will also need to be capable of high resolution. Most office users will spend their time viewing and working with text. They need a monitor that is large enough to view their work clearly, but that doesn't take up too much room on their desk, so TFT monitors may be more practical.

Where is it going to be viewed?

Many people need to view their computer output on the move, via a laptop, PDA or mobile phone. In this situation, the size of display becomes extremely important. Large screens are more comfortable to work with, but much less convenient to carry around. In some respects, this problem refers back to the previous one of what needs to be viewed. Short e-mails, brief notes or websites configured for WAP access will be fine viewed on a small screen, such as a mobile phone. If complex documents need to be created or edited, most people would find that difficult on a screen much smaller than that of a laptop. PDAs are something of a compromise. They allow documents to be created or edited, though most people would not want to spend too much time working in this way. Satellite navigation systems need screens that are large enough to be visible by the driver without obstructing their view of the road, and need mounting devices to support them.

If the monitor is to be used in greasy or dirty situations, such as a food outlet or factory, the monitor may need to be protected from its environment. Some monitors, particularly TFT monitors are not very clear in bright light, or if the user needs to view them at an angle rather than sitting straight in front of them.

Who is going to view the image?

The factors discussed above are mostly considering a screen that is going to be used by one person with normal eyesight. Partially sighted users may require a bigger screen than usual so that they can see more of the page at once on high-zoomed settings, and may find the contrast settings on some monitors better than others.

AQA Examiner's tip

If a question asks you for the **output** from a system, it is asking for the information that is produced by it, for instance a chart showing candidate numbers and marks, rather than the **output device**, for example a laser printer.

If the image is going to be shown to a lot of people at once, in a classroom or lecture hall, a digital projector, perhaps with the use of an interactive whiteboard, is a useful output method.

If a large image is needed on an exhibition stand or in the lobby of a business, a plasma screen may be a better alternative. This also gives the possibility of displaying many different images in the same space by having multiple screens. These could be used to display a slideshow of still images (like a large digital photo frame), or programmes from many different TV channels in the lobby of a TV company.

Fig. 2.5 *Company lobby with multiple screens*

Internet access

When a web designer posts pages on a web server, they usually have no control over who has access to them and what equipment they use to view them. It is extremely important that they consider a wide range of output devices when designing their webpages. They themselves may have very large, high-resolution monitors, and a webpage that looks fine on their display may not work nearly as well on a smaller monitor or one set to a lower resolution or displaying fewer colours. It may be completely impossible to view properly on a PDA or mobile phone. The web designer has to make some decisions about what the minimum specification is that they are going to design to. Designing to 800 × 600 pixels in 256 colours may be a pretty safe set of design parameters, but it can restrict the design possibilities and most users have much better equipment, so the designer may decide to accept that some people will not be able to view the pages properly. This does, however, restrict their potential audience. Many mobile phone companies have their own web portals that allow their customers to view webpages that have been designed with mobile screen sizes in mind. Other sites may have text-only versions that load more quickly and display using less space because there are no graphics to display.

■ Printers

Most users need a printer to produce paper-based output from their computer. Larger organisations may need several printers of different types.

What is to be printed?

If the print output is mainly black text, then a monochrome laser printer is probably the best alternative. They produce high-quality text quickly and the running costs are usually lower than an inkjet, particularly for the more powerful machines. Their output on black and white and greyscale graphics is generally good too.

If colour is used frequently, the choice is really between an inkjet and a colour laser. Either of these could be used instead of a monochrome laser or in addition, for when colour is needed. The laser will generally cost more to buy than the inkjet, but costs less to run. It will produce good quality text and diagrams, but is not so good for photographs. Inkjets tend to be popular for home use, where printing tends to be a mixture of all kinds of documents, and volumes tend to be low. Inkjet photo printers and solid ink printers can produce excellent quality photographs.

How many documents?

The volume of documents to be printed can have a significant effect on the choice of printer. High volumes are handled much more quickly by laser printers, and they also have much bigger paper trays so that they do not need to be filled up as often. Some laser printers come with a built-in network interface card, which is much less common on inkjet printers. This means that they can be used by any machine on the network that has the correct printing permissions. More expensive printers, sometimes called workgroup printers, are designed with more robust components, making them suitable for much higher usage than domestic printers. They can have multiple paper trays for different types of media, and built-in duplex units that can produce double-sided printing automatically. They also tend to have lower running costs than cheaper printers, but they are expensive to buy in the first place, so some companies lease them rather than buy them outright.

What kind of media?

The size and type of media to be printed on needs to be considered. Most printers are designed to be used mostly with A4 paper. Larger paper sizes than this need larger printers, which tend to be expensive, particularly above A3 size. For most people it would be cheaper to have the occasional large copy produced commercially at a print shop rather than buy a larger printer. The thickness of the paper also needs to be considered. Most printers will print on thin card, but it may need to be fed in sheet by sheet.

Most printers can also handle envelopes, though some are more reliable at feeding them through the printer than others, which can be an issue if lots of envelopes need to be printed. Some printers have envelope trays so that the user does not have to change the paper each time they need to print one.

Other common types of media are transparencies and labels. These are available for inkjets and lasers, but it is important to get the correct ones, as they are not interchangeable.

Inkjet printers are generally more versatile regarding specialist media, such as high-gloss papers, textile printing transfers, metallic or plastic films or even special sheets of cotton or silk.

Who is to use the printer?

If the printer is to be shared between multiple users, it will need to be networked. Home networks can share printers, and this is useful as more homes have wireless networks for multiple computers. Many printers can also connect wirelessly to phones and laptops through Bluetooth. Business networks tend to connect the printers through network cards, and have a small number of high-volume printers to cope with the extra load, plus sometimes one or two specialist printers. Network rights can be used to control which users have access to which printers, and software is also available to charge copies to users automatically.

Activity

Look at the website for a company that sells specialist printer products and make a list of which media are available for lasers, and which for inkjets. If the item is available for both, compare the prices to see which work out cheaper.

☑ *In this section you have covered:*

- types of monitor – CRT and TFT
- producing large images through digital projectors or plasma screens
- small screens, such as PDAs and mobile phones and what screen size might mean to the designer
- ways of improving accessibility by adjusting output settings
- things to think about when choosing a display screen:
  - type of data to be viewed – graphics need high resolution, editing large documents is difficult on very small screens, but notes and e-mails need less space
  - space available – TFT screens take up less room than CRT screens, and CRT screens are not practical for portable devices
  - person viewing the display – a large audience will need a large display, perhaps through a digital projector or plasma screen. A partially sighted person will find a large display easier to see
- types of printer – laser, inkjet, dot matrix, solid ink, plotters
- things to think about when choosing a printer:
  - type of output – text, graphics, photographs, monochrome, colour
  - type of media – paper, card, envelopes, transparencies, specialist media such as T-shirt transfer paper or metallic film
  - size of media – 6 inch by 4 inch photographs, A4 documents, A0 drawings
  - volume of output – laser printers are faster than inkjets and cheaper to run, but tend to cost more to buy
  - cost versus efficiency issues – printers that cost more initially may be designed for a larger print throughput and so are more robust and may also be cheaper to run
- things to think about when choosing speakers:
  - sound to be produced – computer warning sounds, game sound effects, music. Music will tend to need higher-quality speakers
  - who needs to listen – headphones suit personal use, external speakers will have greater volume capacity
  - space available – speakers built into monitors or other devices save space compared to external speakers
  - headphones are more convenient for mobile devices such as MP3 players.

3 Storage

In this section you will cover:

- the situations in which data needs to be stored

- what storage devices are available and what media they use

- how to choose storage methods when designing a solution to a problem.

Remember

The amount of data stored is measured in kilobytes (KB):

- 1 megabyte (MB) is 1,024 KB
- 1 gigabyte (GB) is 1,024 MB
- 1 terabyte (TB) is approximately 1,024 GB.

Key terms

File compression: reducing the size of a file by converting it to a different format.

Backing storage: stores data and program files within the computer.

RAM: main memory where all locations can be read and written to equally quickly.

ROM: memory that cannot be changed; used to hold programs and data when the computer is being booted.

BIOS: Basic Input/Output System.

Removable media: used to store data so that it can be taken away from the computer, such as floppy discs, CDs and flash memory.

3.1 Storage devices and media

Reasons for storing data

Computer users need to store data in a variety of circumstances:

- Basic setup information and operating systems are required for the computer to function.
- Application software needs to be available for the user to carry out tasks.
- Files created by the user need to be stored so that they can be used again.
- Data may need to be transferred from one device to another.
- Backup copies need to be taken in case the original files are lost or have become corrupt.

File compression

One way of reducing the size of files that need to be stored is to **compress** them. Photographs, sound and video files tend to be extremely large if they are stored in an uncompressed format, especially if they are of high resolution. A TIFF file created by scanning a photograph will take up much less space if it is converted to a JPEG format, although it will lose some quality when it is compressed. MPEG is a compressed format used for high-quality video images.

It is also possible to use compression utilities to compress any large file, particularly when transmitting it to another computer, either electronically via the Internet or via a storage device. The file is compressed by the sender and then uncompressed by the person who receives it. Compression reduces transmission time or allows more data to be fitted on to any storage medium.

Backup software also compresses the data that is being stored.

Types of storage

Internal and external storage

When a personal computer boots up, it uses data stored in **ROM** to load the **BIOS** to make the computer work. It then loads the operating system software from the hard drive. Applications software and data files are called up from the hard drive as the user requests them. The hard disk and ROM are both inside the computer, so they are internal devices.

In addition to the immediate storage capacity of ROM and **RAM,** a computer needs **backing storage** for mass storage of data and programs.

Most personal computers also make use of a variety of **removable media.** External hard drives which connect through the USB port are also available. DAT tape is often used to back up servers.

Magnetic storage

Hard disks and floppy discs work by storing data on magnetised surfaces.

■ Remember

It is important to remember that the storage *medium* is the surface on which the data is stored. The storage *device* is the hardware that reads the data; for example, a DVD rewriter is the device that reads and writes data to DVD media.

■ Key terms

Mirrored drives: multiple copies of stored data in case the main drive fails.

RAID (redundant array of inexpensive disks): a set of hard disks used to minimise the chances of data loss.

Hot swap: drive can be removed and replaced without shutting down the server, avoiding down time that can interrupt the operation of the organisation.

■ Did you know?

Computer forensic specialists are employed by the police to recover data from encrypted, damaged or deleted files. This includes looking in areas of the hard drive that are usually inaccessible, such as unallocated space on a disk, that while currently unused, may have previously been used to store data.

AQA Examiner's tip

Never choose floppy discs as an answer to a question asking you to recommend a backup medium. They hold very little data and much more suitable methods are available.

Hard disks

Most of the day-to-day storage on PC systems is carried out by the hard disk. A hard disk is made up of rotating plastic or metal disks covered with a magnetic coating on which the data is stored. Read/write heads move between the disks as they spin to read the data from the surfaces. Hard disks are available with very large storage capacities at a relatively low cost. They are fast to read, extremely reliable and robust.

Removable hard drives are useful for extra storage, backup and moving large amounts of data (e.g. video files) from one machine to another.

Computers often have many hard disks rather than just one. **RAID** drives are sets of disks that work together. Each disk can be used to store part of the data. If one drive fails, the other drives automatically take over and the data remains available for the network to use without any network down time. **Mirrored drives** can be set up so that more than one copy of the data exists in case of drive failure. In servers they can usually be **hot swapped**.

For a computer to work efficiently it needs to have quite a lot of space left on its hard drive after current data and programs have been stored. If the drive does not have space to store a large data file in one place, it will split it up and store it in chunks, and the drive becomes fragmented. This slows down access speeds. Hard drive space is also used to store data when the main memory has to do a lot of work, perhaps if the user is multi-tasking. How much space is needed will depend on the task being performed, but if there is not enough space, the performance of the computer will slow right down.

Fig. 3.1 *Hard disk drive*

Floppy discs

Floppy discs were once an extremely popular method of storage, but only hold 1.44 MB of data – no longer a practical storage method – and most new computers do not come with a floppy disc drive as standard any more. They store data on a circular piece of magnetic film, built into a plastic case for protection. They are easily damaged and not very reliable.

DAT tapes

These tapes are small in size but can hold a lot of data. They are often used to back up servers because they are easy to take away and store at a different location to the server. They are quite slow to write to and very slow to retrieve data. They are less reliable than hard drives and more difficult to restore selected files from, but they are a useful removable backup medium.

Optical storage

Optical storage devices such as CDs (compact discs) and DVDs (digital video discs) use optical technology to etch the data onto a plastic-coated metal disc. Laser beams are then passed over the surface to read the data. Both types of disc look the same, but DVDs hold about 4.7 GB of data, whereas CDs hold about 650 MB. DVD drives usually read CDs as well as DVDs. Blu-ray technology is also optical, and offers very large storage capacities.

CD-ROMs and DVD-ROMs are read only – they are often used to supply software. No further data can be written to them.

CD-Rs and DVD-Rs can have data written to them once, but the storage space cannot then be overwritten with new data. They are useful for backing up files and making archive copies of files that are unlikely to be needed but should not be thrown away altogether.

CD-RW and DVD-RW discs can have data written to them many times rather than just once, with the new data overwriting the old. They can be used to transfer data between machines, as they are reusable, but most people tend to find flash drives more convenient for this purpose.

Burning data using CD or DVD drives usually needs special software that formats the disc and copies the data. It then verifies that the data has been copied properly and is readable, warning the user of any errors. It is possible to buy CD and DVD copiers that make several copies at once.

> **AQA** Examiner's tip
>
> If a question asks you to choose a medium to save data to, make sure you choose a CD-R or CD-RW rather than a CD-ROM, because CD-ROMs are read only. The same applies to DVDs.

| CD-ROM – read only | CD-R – write once, then read only | CD-RW – read and write many times |

Fig. 3.2 *Optical storage*

Flash memory

Flash memory, because of its small size, tends to be used for portable devices such as digital cameras, MP3 players, mobile phones and satellite navigation systems. It uses solid-state technology to store data on tiny cards of various types. Flash-based pen drives have become popular as devices for transferring data between machines. They consist of flash memory built into a case with a USB connection, and most operating systems will recognise the drive and allow data to be transferred without installing drivers. Solid-state memory is increasingly being used as the main storage medium in laptops and other portable devices.

■ Did you know?

The capacity of flash memory is increasing rapidly and it is likely to become the standard type of memory used in portable devices in the near future.

Online storage

The increased upload and download speeds made possible by broadband Internet connections has meant that it is now feasible for more people to store their data away from their own computer. Some photograph printing companies offer sites where users can store their photographs. Section 14 will explain the use of online backups.

■ End of sub-topic questions

1. Name three devices that use flash memory as a storage medium. Give three reasons why flash memory has become such a popular medium compared to CD-based storage.

2. Online backup has become a possibility for home users, largely due to fast broadband connections. Give one reason why a family might decide to use online storage to back up their home computer and one area of concern they might have about using such a facility.

💡 3.2 Choosing a storage device

Hard disks – fixed storage

PCs and laptops need hard disks, so the decision in this case is how large the hard disk should be. Hard disk capacities increase so rapidly, it is not easy to give figures, as they quickly become out of date, but an entry-level PC from a reputable manufacturer should have a hard disk with the capacity for the things the average user might want – some word processing and spreadsheet files, photographs and e-mail perhaps, plus the software to create and edit them. In addition to this, there needs to be space for the operating system. All software packages list as part of their specification the minimum hard disk space you need to have free in order to install it.

A user downloading lots of music or video material is likely to need much more hard disk space for storage than the average user and a user who edits video will need even more space, as video creates extremely large files. The final version of a video will usually be compressed, but the uncompressed file will be needed while editing is taking place. For example, if you had two hours of raw footage shot in DV video (data rate = 3,000 Kb/sec), your raw footage would require at least 360–400 MB of storage space.

If an existing computer does not have enough hard disk space, several options are available:

■ Replace the existing hard disk with a larger one.

■ Add a second internal hard disk to store some of the data.

■ Use a removable hard disk, connected via the USB port. This is particularly useful if the original computer is a laptop or the extra hard disk space is not always going to be needed. This option also allows the data to be stored away from the original machine, making it useful for backup purposes.

When buying a new computer, the best rule is probably to buy a machine with a hard disk that is bigger than you think you need.

Activity

Look at an online shop or magazine that allows you to specify the components you want in your machine. Write down the disk size and price for a basic, entry-level machine and then work out the price for machines with bigger hard disks. How much difference does it make to the cost of the overall machine if you choose a hard disk that is twice or three times as big? One way of doing that would be to work out the cost per GB of storage by dividing the cost of the extra space by the added cost above the basic system.

Removable storage

When choosing removable storage, it is important to think about

- the volume of data to be stored
- the reason the data is being stored
- whether data will need to be rewritten
- speed of recovery
- physical size of device.

Archive storage

Some computer users regularly remove data from their hard drive, but make a copy of it on removable media in case they need it at a later date. This archive storage has to be reliable, but will only be used occasionally, so speed of access is not really important. A removable hard disk would be an expensive way of doing this, and flash media is only really intended for short-term storage. Depending on the volume of data, a CD-R or DVD-R, Blu-ray or HD DVD would probably be the best option. They are small and easy to store, but it is important to label them clearly because one unlabelled disc looks very much like another. They are inexpensive to buy, and the data does not need to be overwritten, so RW discs are unlikely to be needed.

Transferring files

A great deal of file transfer goes on via e-mail attachments or sending files through instant messaging services. However, if there is no high-speed connection available, transferring files can be slow and expensive. Even on a broadband link, very large files can be time-consuming to transfer. If the files are to be transferred to a computer without Internet access, a physical medium needs to be used.

Flash memory is convenient because its small physical size makes it very portable, and large capacity memory cards are widely available. Flash pen drives make it easy to transfer data between computers through the USB port, and many printers and laptops have media readers that can accept a variety of card types. Once the file has been transferred, it can be deleted to make room for new data.

Optical discs can also be useful, particularly if the data needs to be sent out to many people. The fact that they are then read-only can be useful in some instances. These discs can also be read by other devices such as CD and DVD players, so they may be particularly appropriate for music, movies and photographs, as the end user does not need to have a computer to view or listen to them.

Removable hard drives can be useful for transferring large files.

Backup

Any storage medium used for backup needs to be extremely reliable as it may be the only way of recovering data if the original copy is stolen or corrupted. Floppy discs are too small to be seriously considered, and flash media is not usually considered suitable for backup storage because it is physically small and vulnerable to damage. That really leaves tape drives, optical media and extra hard drives.

Most domestic users have a relatively small amount of data that needs to be backed up, and much of that data does not change very often. Optical write discs have enough capacity for many people, especially if only the files that have been changed are backed up. Rewritable discs can be used but are slower to write data to.

Removable hard drives are another possible option, with each backup stored as a separate file named by the date it was taken, so that many backups can be stored on one disk. In case of theft or physical damage through fire or flood, the hard drive should be stored away from the main computer, which may mean in practice that two drives are needed if at any time one is to be stored away from the computer.

Many home users now have more than one computer, and may take a backup of the contents of the main PC on the laptop and vice versa using a wireless connection.

Mobile phones and PDAs can also be backed up to a PC or laptop hard disk.

Business users are likely to have a much greater volume of data, often with a high commercial value. RAID drives are likely to be used in servers, with mirrored drives for instant backup, but DAT tape drives are often used as an extra backup medium because they have a large capacity in a format that allows them to be removed and stored elsewhere. The tapes need to be replaced on a regular basis, as they are subject to wear and tear.

Section 14 will discuss backup in greater detail.

■ **End of sub-topic questions**

3 A keen amateur photographer owns the following storage media:

- removable hard disk
- CD-R
- flash memory.

Describe a possible use the photographer could make of each type of medium listed.

☑ *In this section you have covered:*

- reasons for storing data:
  - programs and data for future use
  - transferring data to another location
  - archiving and backup
- most computers use hard drives for storage of data and programs (fixed storage) plus a variety of removable storage methods for backup and transferring data

- types of storage medium:
  - magnetic (hard and floppy discs, DAT tape)
  - optical (CD, DVD, Blu-ray and HD DVD)
  - solid state (flash memory cards and USB sticks)
- optical memory can be read only (e.g. CD-ROM), write once (CD-R) or write many (CD-RW)
- strengths and weaknesses of each type, including physical size, storage capacity, access speed and reliability
- common uses for each type of medium
- things to think about when choosing a storage method:
  - volume of data – floppy discs store very little, CDs less than DVDs. Blu-ray and HD DVD more than DVD. DAT tape, flash memory and hard disks hold most, and are available with different storage capacities. Removable hard disks are available
  - purpose of storage – transfer of data is most convenient on small media such as flash memory sticks, CD-R and DVD-Rs; this tends to be less important for backup, although a copy of data needs to be stored elsewhere. Flash memory is not generally considered suitable for backup
  - need for re-writing – this is not possible on CD-R and DVD-R, as they can only be written to once
  - speed of recovery of data – hard drives have quick access and mirrored drives can take over instantly if the main drive fails; CD and DVD media are slower to read from; DAT tape is more difficult to retrieve individual files from
  - size of device – flash memory is most suitable for portable or small devices such as mobile phones, MP3 players and some laptops.

4 Software

In this section you will cover:

■ operating system software and why it is needed

■ the main types of applications software available for problem solving

■ how to choose software when designing a solution to a problem.

The term 'software' covers the program commands that make a computer do the tasks we need it to do, and we usually refer to them as software packages. Computer systems need two main types of software – systems software and applications software. The main piece of systems software is the operating system, which is needed to make the electronic components of the computer work usefully and efficiently. Applications software, for example a word processor, is needed for users to carry out the various tasks that they wish to perform on the computer.

4.1 Systems software

The operating system controls the system hardware including memory, processor time and storage. Some of its main functions include:

■ managing memory when the computer is carrying out more than one task

■ allocating processor time between the various processes being carried out

■ controlling where data is stored on disk

■ communicating with input and output devices

■ handling errors and displaying error messages

■ system security, user and file permissions.

When computers are multi-tasking, they appear to be doing many jobs at once, but in fact processor time needs to be allocated to each of the jobs, some of which need to be given priority. Newer processors with multiple cores make this easier, as they act as if the computer has more than one

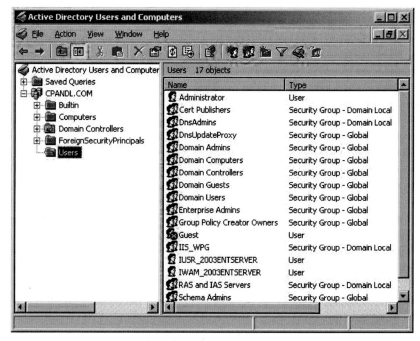

Fig. 4.1 *Network operating system*

processor, but the operating system still has to manage how tasks are to be carried out.

The operating system is also responsible for providing the end-user interface, usually a graphical user interface or GUI.

Any application software used on a computer needs to be compatible with the operating system being used. Microsoft Windows and Apple's Mac OS X are the most common operating systems for personal computers, though there is considerable support for LINUX, a free operating system developed by volunteers. UNIX was originally developed for large computers, and still tends mostly to be used in large server type systems as it allows software to be used over a range of hardware platforms.

Networked computers need a network operating system to handle user rights, file permissions and communication between computers.

End of sub-topic questions

1 All computers need an operating system. Explain why this is so, using three functions of an operating system to justify your answer.

2 Network operating systems perform functions over and above a standard operating system. Describe two functions of a network operating system.

Utility software carries out some of the basic tasks the user needs to perform. Some of these utilities, such as file management, may be built into the operating system, others, such as anti-virus software may be purchased separately. Other examples of utility software are firewalls, disk cleanup, defragmentation and backup software.

4.2 Applications software

Applications software is the software with which users process text, numbers, still and moving images and sound. Some packages process more than one type of medium, and are referred to as multimedia software.

Text

Most software packages, including spreadsheet, database management and graphics packages will have basic text-processing functions, including:

- choice of fonts, such as Times New Roman or Arial
- font sizes and colours
- font styles, such as italic, bold and underline
- ability to use text as art by changing its shape and adding artistic effects
- aligning text to the left, right or centre or fully justifying it.

These functions can be useful for emphasising headings or titles, making keywords stand out or to make a page more interesting to look at.

Most packages have built-in facilities to check spelling.

AQA Examiner's tip

When answering questions about software, always remember to use the name of the type of software – for example, a desktop publishing package. Answers that use brand names, such as Microsoft Publisher will not be awarded marks.

Word processing

Most business computer time is still devoted to word processing, and so word processors have to be versatile tools. Whilst it is possible to add graphics and other objects to word-processed documents, most of the functions of a word processor are dedicated to the text itself.

Templates and wizards

Word-processing packages usually come with a range of templates for many types of standard document such as letters, invoices and reports. They can be customised to suit the needs of the organisation without having to design the document from scratch. Some templates may have extra functions, such as built-in calculations of totals for invoices, or links to a customer database for easy mail merging.

Wizards allow the user more control over the document as it is being created, allowing them to make changes of layout, font and colours as they go along. The final document can still be customised.

If standard templates are used, there is a danger that documents produced will look very similar to those of other people; it is important to customise them to produce a house style. Once the templates have been finalised, all new documents can be based on them, giving a consistent look to the whole range.

Proofing tools

As well as spell checking, most word processors have other functions to improve the quality of the language – grammar checking, thesaurus, word count and level-of-language analysis tools.

Styles

Styles help to keep the document consistent. If a heading is in Arial font size 14 bold, setting a heading style means this can be applied to all headings of the same level, saving time if changes need to be made to the style, and making mistakes less likely. Tables of contents can be automatically built using these styles.

Layout tools

Basic tools such as columns and tables, background watermarks, borders and shading are available in most packages. Key words can be marked so that an index is automatically created, and footnotes can also be setup if necessary. Fields can be used to add page numbers or other details such as file name and location automatically.

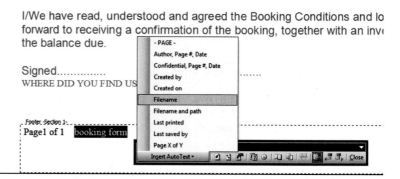

Fig. 4.2 *Fields are automatically updated*

Shared projects/track changes

Long documents such as books and reports are often worked on by teams of people, and it can be difficult to keep track as people add their contributions. Word-processing software can be set to track changes. Once the original document has been produced, it is passed to other people for comments and editing. The changes and comments they make appear in a different colour. The original author can see both versions and then accept or reject the changes.

Days Worked

ID	Title	Forename	Surname	Occupation	Extension Number	Days Worked
BHC 01	Dr	James	Brown	Senior Partner	111	Every Day
BHC 02	Mrs	Keith	McDonald	Practice Nurse	102	Tues, Thurs
BHC 03	Mr	David	Smith	Practice Nurse	102	Mon, Wed, Fri
BHC 04	Dr	Sanjit	Singh	Practitioner	103	Every Day
BHC 05	Miss	Kay	Rogan	CPN	105	Tues, Wed
BHC 06	Dr	Judith	Battersby	Senior Partner	104	Mon-Thu
BHC 07	Miss	Paula	Adams	Secretary	110	Every Day
BHC 08	Miss	Hayley	Cropper	Receptionist	107	Mon-Wed
BHC 09	Mrs	Mary	Taylor	Receptionist	107	Thu, Fri
BHC 10	Dr	Sara	Cheung	Practitioner	109	Wed-Fri
BHC 11	Mrs	Paula	Adams	Practice Manager	100	Every Day
BHC 12	Mr	Carl	Smith	Psychotherapist	108	Mon, Wed, Fri
BHC 13	Mrs	Claudia	Price	Secretary	110	Tues, Thu, Fri
BHC 14	Dr	Satnam	Singh	Senior Partner	113	Tues-Fri
BHC 15	Ms	Rosalina	Leonetti	CPN	105	Mon, Fri
BHC 16	Mrs	Jenny	Smythe	Receptionist	107	Every Day
BHC 17	Dr	Juergen	Kessler	Practitioner	112	Every day
BHC 18	Mr	Nick	Guy	Receptionist	107	Every Day

Comment [DES1]: Surely this can't be right?

Deleted: Cheng

Deleted: Smith

Fig. 4.3 *Document with track changes being used*

On-screen forms

If the user has to enter data into a table or form, it is possible to set up on-screen prompts or dialogue boxes so that they avoid having to navigate between fields and the data is automatically entered in the correct place.

Desktop publishing

Desk top publishing (DTP) packages concentrate on the layout of the document rather than just the text, and tend to have a wider range of templates such as leaflets, brochures, business cards, DVD and CD inserts. Each object on the page is enclosed in a frame which can be dragged around the page, resized, rotated or arranged in layers. Grids, distribution and alignment tools can help to keep designs lined up accurately.

DTP packages can be used to produce electronic output, such as websites, but their main purpose is for decorative paper-based documents. Templates and wizards can form a starting point and simple drawing tools are available.

Database management software

The data stored in most databases is usually largely text, although numbers, pictures and sound files can also be stored. A **flat file database** is a single table that stores data **records** that are arranged in **fields**.

Data types

Database fields can be text, numbers, date/time, or logical (yes/no). Calculated fields can be set up based on the values in other fields.

Key terms

Flat file database: is a single table that stores data records arranged in fields.

Record: a set of data relating to an individual or object.

Field: a single category of data within a record.

Validation

It is extremely important that data-entry errors are reduced as for as possible. More information about validation is available in Section 6 of this book on pp63–4.

Sorts

Stored records can be sorted by any field and in ascending or descending order.

Queries

The most powerful function of a database is the ability to query the data against certain **criteria**. If a mobile phone company keeps its contract details on a database they could search:

- one field, for instance all customers with monthly contracts
- two fields, for instance all customers with monthly contracts on a particular network
- by using calculations, for instance all customers who have contracts due to expire within the next month.

■ **Key terms**

Criteria: used to define database queries, such as 'Show all product numbers with sales over £2,000 last month'.

■ **Remember**

A database table is made up of records, one for each person or item data is being stored about. Each record is made up of fields that can be of a variety of data types.

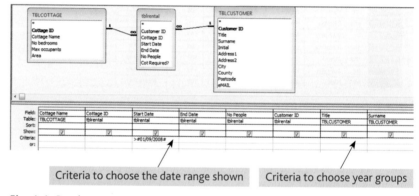

Fig. 4.4 *Database query*

Forms

Most database management packages have powerful form design functions so that the user interface is made as easy to use as possible for entering and viewing data. Wizards can produce a basic form layout which can then be customised to meet the user's requirements, perhaps by matching an existing paper-based form or to bring the form in line with house style.

Reports

Printed data is usually better viewed via a report. Again, a wizard may be useful to create the basic report, which can then be adjusted to suit the user. Calculated fields can be very useful in reports, for example to calculate the total sales figures for each sales representative as a percentage of the total sales for a given month.

Relational database management systems

Relational databases are created by linking two or more tables through a primary key field. Each table stores data about one **entity**. This can reduce the amount of data entered and stored, which improves the integrity of the data. For example, if a cottage rental business has details

■ **Key terms**

Relational database: stores data in tables that are linked together through primary keys. A primary key provides a unique identifier for each field.

Entity: a thing about which data is held in a database.

of cottages and customers, it would be time consuming to type in full details of every cottage rented by each customer, as many customers will book more than one pental. If each customer and each cottage are given a unique reference code, the data can be linked via a third table called rental, which has the customer code, the cottage code, and the dates booked. This means that when a customer books another holiday, their details are already stored in the system, and will not need to be entered again. It also makes sure that if the customer changes their details, perhaps by moving house, the changes only need to be made once, and it will automatically be reflected in each of their bookings.

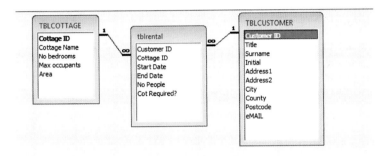

Fig. 4.5 *Structure of the cottage rental database*

Relational database management software is powerful, because queries can be made across tables, so it would be easy to create:

- a form that shows all the holiday bookings made by one customer, so that if they ring with a query, all their details are together
- a report that shows all the bookings for an individual cottage arranged by date, so that the cleaners know when they will be needed
- a report that gives all bookings for a particular month and calculates the total income for that month to help predict cash flow.

Numbers

Whilst spreadsheets are the most obvious software for processing numbers, databases often have advanced calculation options too, although calculated fields and queries can be more complex to set up. Calculated fields can also be set into word-processed documents to do simple calculations such as totals on an invoice.

Spreadsheets

Spreadsheets have many built-in formulas and functions for processing numbers for various purposes, such as:

- mathematics and trigonometry – tangent, sine, cosine, rounding, random numbers, etc.
- finance – interest calculations, depreciation, future values, etc.
- date and time – calculations on dates can be carried out; today's date can be generated automatically and used in calculations
- statistics – mean, standard deviation, distributions, etc.
- lookup and database functions – maximum and minimum values, counts and extracting values from tables.

Remember

It is much cheaper to make bad decisions on a computer model than it is to make them in real life. Exploring the possibilities by modelling can help organisations avoid expensive mistakes.

Spreadsheet models can be used to explore the possible effects of changes, answering 'What if?' questions. For instance, a financial model could calculate answers to such questions as:

- What would be the effect on annual costs if interest rates went up by 1 per cent for 3 months and dropped back down after that?
- It costs us more to put on extra operators but customers won't wait for too long, so what is the minimum number of checkouts we have to have open at quiet times and at busy ones?

Scenarios can be set up, so that the managers of the company can base their decisions on reliable information. It can often be useful to present information using charts, and spreadsheets have a large range of chart types for this purpose.

Pictures

Pictures can be used to explain things, to make pages look attractive or to draw attention to a particular area.

There are two main types of graphics software – bitmap and vector.

Bitmap software

Bitmap images are made by splitting the screen into tiny squares, called **pixels**. The colour of each pixel is stored, and images made up of lots of colours create large file sizes. Low-resolution images are made up of a small number of large pixels, whereas high-resolution images have more pixels, each of which is smaller, giving higher quality but larger file sizes. If a bitmap image is enlarged, each pixel is made bigger, which reduces quality and tends to make the edges jagged.

Bitmap software tends to be used for freehand art and for photographs. There are general-purpose graphics packages, packages that specialise in art and those that are designed to edit photographs. Many of the functions will be similar, but each will have specialist functions such as

Key terms

Pixel: a single, usually square, dot that makes up a bitmap image.

Fig. 4.6 *Pixellation caused by over-enlargement*

red-eye removal for photographs. The range of functions of some bitmap packages can make them difficult for beginners to use, so many scanners and digital cameras come with cut-down packages designed to allow non-specialists to crop and edit their photographs, adjust brightness and contrast and remove the red-eye effect caused by flash bouncing off the subject's eyes.

Good-quality art packages have a range of tools, so that strokes can look like paint or chalk, ink or lines of stars. They will also have filters that can make a sketch look like an oil painting, a watercolour or a psychedelic masterpiece. The software uses layers so that each section of the image can be worked on without affecting the others. Selecting areas of the image can be difficult, and there are various tools to do that.

 Activity

Most computers come with a simple bitmap editing package included. Make a list of the main functions included with that package. Make a similar list for any other packages you might have available, such as photo editing or a more general art package. Write a short report that compares the functions of each package, including how easy each one is to learn to use.

Vector software

Vector graphics are made up of objects, each of which can be selected so that it can be filled, edited, moved or resized. The shape of each object is plotted mathematically, and the quality is not affected if the image is resized. Objects can be grouped together so that they move and resize as if they were one object. Objects can also be layered on top of each other. Vector images tend to be used for diagrams, and computer-aided design packages tend to be vector based. In general, vector images tend to have smaller file sizes than bitmaps because only the objects have to be defined, whereas bitmaps have to define the colour of every pixel on the page. Many packages combine bitmap fills with vector outlines to give a more realistic texture to vector objects. Vector graphics are sometimes limited as to which software can be used to view them.

Some computer-aided design packages enable designers to draw objects in 2D and have them converted to 3D wireframes. Skins can be added to make the object look realistic, and the object can be rotated and viewed from any angle. This allows designers to experiment with the look of a product without having to make expensive models and prototypes.

Key terms

Vector: graphics that store the instructions for drawing each object on the page, rather than the picture as a whole.

Moving images

Moving images are actually made up from sequences of still images that are played back at a speed that is fast enough to trick the human eye into thinking they are moving. Video footage does that by recording a series of still photographs with a camera; animations do the same thing with drawn images.

Video-editing software

Footage recorded on a digital video camera can be loaded on to a computer to be edited. Sections of the video can be removed or cut and pasted, rather like words in a word-processing package. Photo-editing software functions, such as adjusting brightness are also available for video. Captions and titles can be added, and important points marked so that the user can jump between sections when they play the video. Sound files, such as music or spoken commentary, can also be played alongside the images, and some producers use animation sequences with recorded video for special effects or to add novelty. Video files can be extremely large, and video software can use compression to reduce the size of the files, but if the video is compressed too much the image quality will be reduced.

Animation software

Animation involves drawing lots of individual frames that are then displayed in sequence to give the illusion of movement. This would be very time consuming, so animation software has the facility to carry out 'in betweening', where the objects are drawn in their starting and ending positions, and the computer draws the frames in between. The designer can choose how many frames are inserted. A larger number of frames gives a smoother movement, but increases the file size. The playback speed can also be controlled to make the object move faster or slower.

Short animations are often recorded as GIF files to add movement to webpages, and it is important that the file sizes are kept very low to avoid increasing download times too much.

Did you know?

The film stock on which some old movies were originally recorded has proved not to age very well, and the colours on it are breaking down. Some classic movies have been edited frame by frame to remove spots and other faults and to restore the original brighter colours.

Fig. 4.7 *Animation*

Sound

Software for working with sound tends to fall into two categories – sound editing and music composition. Sound editing works with the waveforms generated by the sounds, music composition with musical notation.

Sound editing

As explained in Section 1, sound files are created by taking samples of sounds and playing them back. Higher sampling rates generate better-quality sounds but larger files. Sound-editing software can change the shape of the waveforms, making the sound higher or lower in pitch or volume, or changing the pattern of the waves to make them sound different. It is also possible to cut and paste sections of the sound waves, so a missing word could be inserted, or a note the singer didn't quite reach could magically be improved.

Sound effects for theatres can be created by mixing and editing sounds, so that they produce the desired effect and are easy to play back. For instance, a spooky play might open with three owl hoots and the clanging of a church bell. The wave sequence for the owl hoot would be pasted in three times, followed by that of the church bell. The whole sequence is then given a number which is called up by the sound desk whenever it is required.

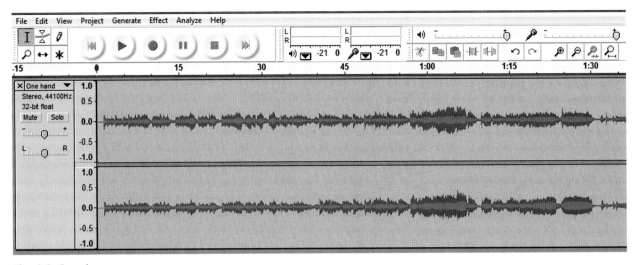

Fig. 4.8 *Sound sequence*

The ability to mix sounds also makes it possible for performers to record tracks separately and then play them back together. The separate tracks make editing easier.

Music composition

Writing music by drawing individual notes on music manuscript paper is extremely time consuming, and the results can be difficult to read. Music composition software makes this task a great deal easier.

Input method

Notes can be dragged from a library and placed in the correct position on the stave, or they can be fed in from a digital instrument such as a

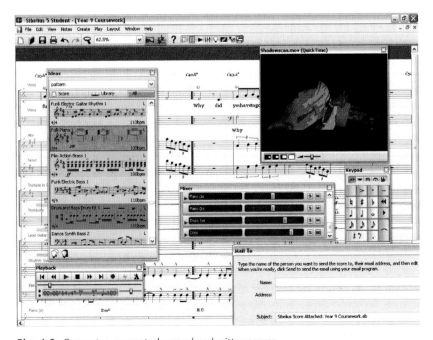

Fig. 4.9 *Computer-generated versus handwritten scores*

keyboard via MIDI (musical instrument digital interface), allowing the musician to compose by playing rather than writing.

Editing

Once the music has been entered, it can be played back in any 'voice', so a sound that has been entered via a keyboard can be played back to sound like a violin, for example. Errors can be corrected and improvements made until the composer is happy with the finished piece, which can then be printed out as a tidy musical score that is easy to follow, rather like musical word processing. Lyrics can be added to the score with each word lining up neatly with the note at which it is sung.

Advanced composition software also has a range of specialist functions, such as the ability to rewrite music in a different key by transposing it automatically, or produce orchestra scores where each instrument is playing a different version of the music to produce harmonies.

■ Multimedia

Some packages concentrate on the process of using various types of data together to provide **multimedia** output. In many cases the output is also **interactive**, rather than passive.

Presentation software

Multimedia presentations can be used, for example, in:

- lectures and lessons presented to a group via a screen or interactive whiteboard
- training material designed for the user to work through at their own pace on a computer
- advertising presentations in shopping centres and at exhibitions
- customer information booths in shops and shopping centres.

Generally speaking, these presentations will use limited amounts of text, relying on the other types of media to convey the message to the audience:

- Pictures can be used to explain concepts and add visual interest.
- Animations can also be used to explain complex procedures and make them easier to understand.
- Videos can make presentations seem more realistic.
- Sound can be used to produce sound effects, background music or spoken commentary.

Which media to use will depend on what type of material is being communicated, who the user is, where they are using the presentation and the artistic effects the presentation is trying to achieve. The choice of media is extremely important to the effect the presentation creates. An animated graphic can be amusing and attract attention, but too many can be irritating and distracting. The same is true of sound effects – they need to be used sparingly.

Presentations generally consist of a series of slides, each one dealing with a fairly small amount of information. If they are being presented by a speaker, they will usually be played in sequence, with the speaker controlling them using a mouse or other pointing device. If the presentation is to play automatically, the user can select the time for

> **Key terms**
>
> **Multimedia:** combined use of different media – text, pictures, moving images and sound.
>
> **Interactive:** gives the user input choices that affect their path through the material.

each slide to be displayed before moving on to the next. Objects within each slide can be animated, appearing after a given length of time and following a particular path. Transitions can also be set, using visual effects to link between screens.

Most packages have a wide range of standard templates available, but these can be customised by changing colours and layouts. Interactive whiteboards come with software that has functions and clip art suitable for educational use.

Web authoring software

It is possible to create webpages on a simple text processor by writing **HTML** code directly, but most designers tend to use packages which create the code from a visual layout. Many word processors, presentation and DTP packages have facilities to save the file as an HTML document, and some have templates for webpages, but the functions they offer are likely to be more restricted than a special-purpose web-design package.

There are many web-design packages available. The more advanced packages tend to have more functions but can be more difficult to use. Style sheets can be created that ensure a consistent look to the site, and templates are available for standard pages such as contact forms. Form controls help the designer to create online forms that are easy to use, and some packages allow a database to be linked to the form so that data collected online is automatically stored to make it easy to analyse.

It is also possible to download sections of code to use on websites, for example to produce visual effects or count visitor numbers.

E-mail software

E-mail software allows the user to store contact details in an address book, and to group some of those contacts together so that an e-mail can be sent to all of them with a single click. Each contact can be allocated

> **Key terms**
>
> **HTML (Hypertext Markup Language):** the language in which webpages are written.

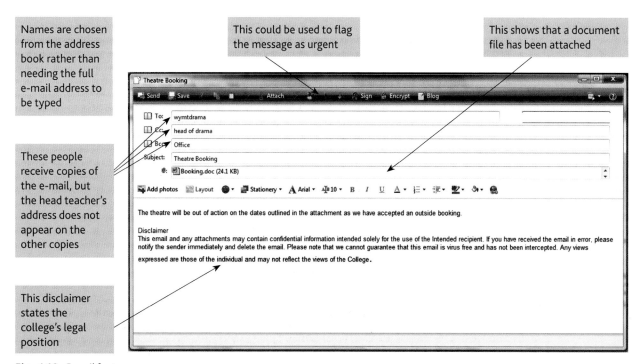

Fig. 4.10 *E-mail features*

Names are chosen from the address book rather than needing the full e-mail address to be typed

This could be used to flag the message as urgent

This shows that a document file has been attached

These people receive copies of the e-mail, but the head teacher's address does not appear on the other copies

This disclaimer states the college's legal position

a short name, which makes it easier to choose the recipient. If a user receives an e-mail, they can use the reply button to send an e-mail back, rather than having to re-type the address of the person who sent it, or forward the e-mail to another by selecting their name from the address book. E-mails can be sent to several people at once by sending a carbon copy (cc) or, if the sender does not want to show who else it is being sent to, by sending a blind carbon copy (bcc).

Rules can be set up to direct incoming mail to a specific folder automatically. Junk mail filters can be used to delete e-mails containing certain words or from a certain address. Many e-mail packages automatically check incoming and outgoing messages for viruses. Flags can be added to important messages so that the person who receives them can see straight away that they are urgent. Electronic signatures or disclaimers can be set to appear at the end of each e-mail that is created.

Web browsers

Web browsers allow users to navigate between intranet pages or internet sites. The user can choose the webpage their browser opens to by setting it as their home page, and newer browsers allow several pages to be loaded at once by using tabbed windows. The back and forward buttons allow the user to go back to pages they have recently visited. The refresh button will reload a page, and the stop button will cancel the loading of a page.

Users can save websites they use frequently to a favourites list – also called bookmarking. They can also bring up a history of the pages that they have viewed previously. Some browsers have extra functions, such as pop-up blockers or the ability to add **RSS feeds** to a personalised home page.

■ **Key terms**

RSS (Really Simple Syndication) feed: allows you to see when websites have added new content as soon as it is published, without having to visit the websites you have taken the feed from.

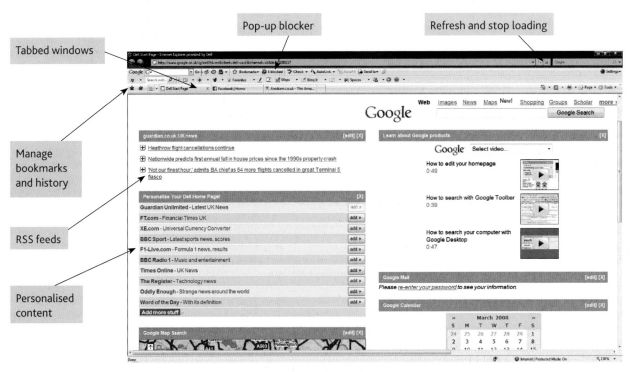

Fig. 4.11 *Tabbed pages in Internet Explorer*

End of sub-topic questions

3 A holiday company wishes to e-mail all its clients about the new destinations they have available for next summer. State three functions of e-mail software they could use that would make this an efficient way of distributing this information.

4 Emma has been carrying out some research for a college project and now needs to build a bibliography of sources she has used. She can no longer remember the name of the main website she used.

Suggest one way she could have made sure that she could find the page at a later date.

Suggest two ways she could find the page again.

4.3 Choosing applications software

The most important factor to consider when choosing applications software is the task that needs to be done. It is extremely important to have a list of end-user requirements so that you can evaluate the strengths and weaknesses of each available piece of software against it.

NAME:

SOFTWARE COMPARISON FOR:

Function	Software: Photo editing package				Software: Full bitmap art package			
	Possible?	Easy to Use?	Mark /10	Comment	Possible?	Easy to Use?	Mark /10	Comment
Red eye reduction	Yes	Very	9	Can even choose eye colour	Yes	No	6	Need to use select tool and then fill

Fig. 4.12 *Software comparison form*

It is important to look carefully at each software package to consider what functions are available and how easy they are to use. Not all functions of the software will be relevant to the task being considered, and they need to be compared with the requirements specification to decide which ones may be needed.

Sometimes the main choice will be between two different types of software package; for instance, spreadsheet versus database management system, word processor versus desktop publishing. At other times the choice will be between two packages of the same type; for instance, two different web authoring packages.

The experience and skill level of the end user can be an important consideration. End users tend to be happier using packages with which they are familiar, although a well-designed solution with a good user interface and user guide may be a better solution if it carries out the task more effectively. One important factor to consider is whether the packages being considered support the use of macros. Macros allow a series of actions to be recorded and played back with a single mouse click or key stroke. They are an important tool for building a simple and efficient user interface.

If existing data needs to be transferred to the new software, the issue of transferability will be important, as the user is unlikely to want to have to re-enter all the data. It is much better if the new software can simply import it.

It may be important that the software is compatible with other software already in use. Desktop publishing packages, for instance, tend to have to use text and picture files created with other packages.

If new software is to be purchased, the overall cost of implementing the solution will rise, especially if the operating system or hardware needs to be upgraded to run the application. This still may be worth considering if it saves a significant amount of time or produces a better solution, but the end user would need to be involved with that decision.

■ Producing documents

The main choice in this instance is usually between a word-processing package and a desktop publishing package, or perhaps between two different packages of the same type. The decision is likely to rest on the type of layout required and whether the user needs complex text-processing tools such as footnotes, tables of content and indexes.

In general, word processors will have more powerful functions for handling text, DTP packages for handling graphics and layouts.

■ Analysing data

Here, the choice is usually between spreadsheets and database management systems. Database management systems tend to have better facilities for end user interfaces, with powerful facilities for creating data entry forms and user navigation, but spreadsheets will generally be better at number crunching using complex formulae.

■ Image production

The choice between vector and bitmap graphics will usually be fairly straightforward, depending on the type of image that needs to be produced. Diagrams and drawings will generally need a vector package, art and photographs a bitmap package.

The choice of which package to use within that image type will largely depend on the complexity of the image being produced. Most application packages can produce simple vector diagrams using standard shapes that can be coloured and layered. A dedicated package will have far more functions, but these will tend to be more difficult to use, so the skill and experience of the user may be a factor to consider.

For editing photographic bitmaps the choice tends to be between a dedicated photo-editing package and a more general art package. A simple photo-editing package will have all the functions needed for cropping images and doing simple improvements like adjusting brightness, but a more advanced package will have specialist tools to create special effects, or to clean up old and damaged photographs by removing cracks and scratches. The more advanced functions take time and need a considerable amount of skill. This may be wasted if the final image is a small, low-resolution picture on a webpage.

Many graphics packages have animation facilities, but it is also possible to buy dedicated animation packages. Again the functions will be more advanced, but the person using the package will need to be prepared to spend time getting to know how they work. The same is true of video editors.

Working with sound

The same general rule applies as with art packages – more complex programs will offer more advanced functions, but tend to be more difficult to use. The decision will rest on whether the advanced functions are really required and how competent the user is in using the software (or how much time they are willing to invest in learning to use it).

Multimedia

The first thing that needs to be considered when choosing a multimedia package is the way in which the final product is to be accessed. Pages designed on a web authoring package can be used on an intranet as well as on the Internet, and could be a valid way of producing information or training materials to be used in this way. They could also be used to illustrate a speech or lesson, although they tend to have fewer functions to allow the speaker to control how the information is presented than a presentation package would have. Interactive whiteboards tend to come with their own software, but are equally capable of presenting slide shows or webpages, and so a close look at the functions of each package will be needed.

Any multimedia package will need to import files produced on other packages, so the compatibility of those other packages and the files they produce will be important.

Again, basic packages will do most of the simple jobs, whereas more specialist packages will have a larger range of functions but may be more complex to use.

End of sub-topic questions

5 Describe the difference between a bitmap image and a vector graphic. Explain where you might use each type of image when illustrating a textbook.

6 You have been asked to solve a data-handling problem by a local company that concerns their stock control. You are not sure whether spreadsheet or database management software would be the more appropriate solution. What questions would you ask the client to help you make your decision?

☑ *In this section you have covered:*

- operating systems software and how it is needed to make the computer function properly

- the functions of an operating system, such as file and memory management, resource allocation, communicating between hardware and software, user permissions and security

- applications software and the way that it is used to carry out useful tasks for users

- applications software for processing text – word processors, desktop publishing packages, databases for data handling

- applications software for processing images – vector software for graphics, bitmap software for photographs and art work, animation and video editing software for moving images

- applications software for processing sound by sampling and editing sound waves. Music composition software for composing musical pieces, editing and transposing them and producing clear, easy-to-read scores

- multimedia packages for processing and combining objects of a variety of media types to make interesting and effective presentations.

5 Health and safety

In this section you will cover:

- the hazards associated with computer use
- the risks associated with these hazards
- precautions that can be taken to reduce the risk.

🔆 5.1 Health and safety of ICT systems

Health and Safety at Work Act

The Health and Safety at Work Act sets out to protect workers from things that could cause them to have accidents or damage their health. Employers have a duty of care to their employees and so they have to assess the risks their workers are exposed to and do their best to keep the risks to a minimum by taking appropriate steps.

Health and safety in any situation is approached by carrying out a risk assessment of the situation. To do this, you should:

- Identify the hazards the user is exposed to.
- Identify the risks those hazards can produce.
- Put safety precautions in place to reduce the risks.
- Train workers to deal with any risks that remain.
- Check regularly to see that the situation has not become worse for any reason.
- Encourage staff to report any health and safety problems that they encounter.

In terms of computer workstations, the best way to carry out the risk assessment is by using a checklist of standards the workstation is expected to meet. This should identify any problems that need to be dealt with. The workstation should then be checked a little while later to make sure the necessary precautions are in place.

Worked example

> Mike Edwards is the safety officer for an ICT consultancy company. When carrying out a risk assessment on a workstation, he notices that the mechanism to adjust the height of the chair is broken. The graphic designer who is not particularly tall, is sitting in an incorrect position that may cause back pain. The company would need to:
>
> - Arrange for the chair to be repaired, or order a new one.
> - Show the operator how to adjust the chair and what position she should be aiming for.
> - Suggest that a foot rest might help to achieve a better posture.
> - Check in a week's time to make sure that the situation has been resolved.
> - Explain to the graphic designer that it is important to report health and safety hazards.

🔆 Display Screen Equipment Regulations

The health and safety regulations that apply to computer use are called the Display Screen Equipment Regulations. It doesn't matter whether the regulations refer to display screens or VDUs, they are designed

AQA Examiner's tip

The examination is only concerned about health and safety issues caused by using computers. Risks created by faulty electrical wiring apply just as much to a photocopier or even a kettle, so should not be used as an answer. In a similar way, poor lighting and ventilation affect all employees and so no marks would be awarded for discussing them. Whilst it is obviously not good practice to take food and drinks near to a computer, the same would be true of a photocopier, so that answer would also not gain marks.

to safeguard people who use computers for long periods of time. The regulations only apply to workers who use computers for a significant part of their working day, although it is obviously good practice to make sure that all workers have safe and comfortable working conditions.

Back pain and spinal damage

People who work on computers spend most of their working day sitting in one position, and this exposes them to the risk of back pain or even permanent spinal damage, particularly if their posture is incorrect.

It is difficult to remove this risk entirely, but by designing workstations correctly the chances of potential health problems can be reduced and good job design improves the situation even more.

Workstation design

Workstations should be **ergonomically** sound. The general principle involved here is that as far as possible the workstation should be adjustable to suit the needs of individual workers. The spine should be kept as straight as possible, with forearms approximately horizontal and eyes at the same level as the top of the monitor. There are several ways of achieving this:

- Chairs should be adjustable in height and provide good back support.
- Monitors should tilt and swivel.
- Keyboards should be adjustable in height.
- There should be enough work space provided for documents and any other equipment needed.
- Document holders may be useful to avoid awkward neck and eye movements.
- Some workers may find a foot rest helpful.
- A wrist rest may also relieve strain on the wrists for some users.

Job design

If at all possible, workloads should be arranged so that workers don't spend long sessions at the keyboard without doing anything else. In many situations it is possible to share duties so that the worker moves around to do other tasks, such as filing or answering the telephone and so changes position. If this is not possible, it is important that workers are allowed to take regular short breaks. The regulations do not specify how often breaks should be taken, and this depends to some extent on the kind of work being done.

Training

It is also important to make sure that workers understand the risks and are trained to reduce them. They need to know what position they should be aiming for and how to adjust the furniture and equipment to achieve it. They should be encouraged to change position regularly by moving and stretching, and organising their work so that they don't spend too long at the computer. When people are busy or have targets to meet, they may be tempted to skip breaks, and they need to understand why it is important to take them.

Repetitive strain injury (RSI)

The Health and Safety Executive tends not to refer to RSI, as the phrase means different things to different people. Instead, they refer to 'upper limb disorders'. Whatever phrase is used, the risk is caused by the fact that people who use computers often perform the same movements over

■ Key terms

Ergonomics: the science of designing equipment to suit the user and help them to work safely.

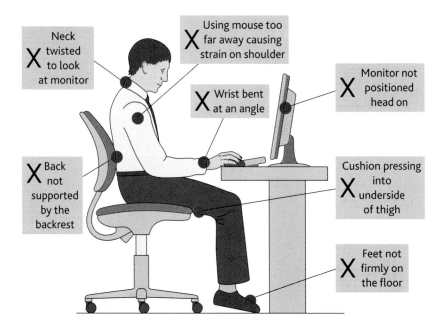

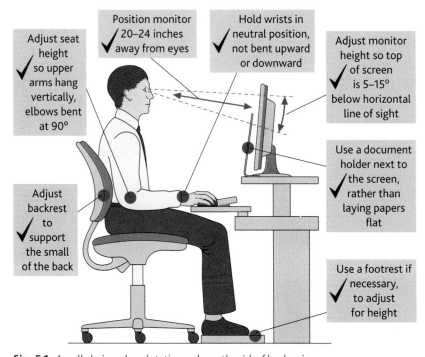

Fig. 5.1 *A well-designed workstation reduces the risk of back pain*

and over again when using a keyboard or mouse, and this can cause pain and damage to joints, sometimes permanently.

Keyboard

Keyboards should be height-adjustable so that the user can find a comfortable keying position. A space in front of the keyboard is useful for resting the hands and wrists when not keying. Users need to be trained to adopt good keying habits, keeping their wrists straight, using a gentle touch on the keys and not over-stretching the fingers. Using an ergonomically designed keyboard can also help.

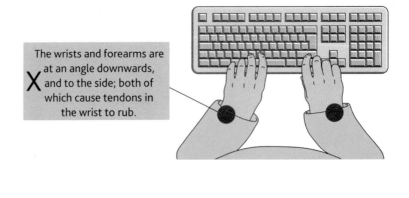

X The wrists and forearms are at an angle downwards, and to the side; both of which cause tendons in the wrist to rub.

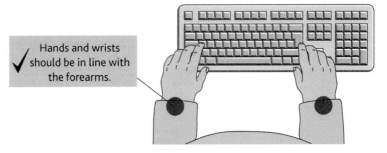

✓ Hands and wrists should be in line with the forearms.

Fig. 5.2 *A good keying position reduces strain on the wrists and fingers*

Mouse

The mouse should be placed so that it is easy to reach and can be used with the wrist straight. The user should sit upright and close to the desk to avoid having to reach too far. Forearms should be supported on the desk, and the mouse should not be gripped too

Fig. 5.3 *Touch screens may help reduce RSI*

tightly. Again, users need to be made aware of this and encouraged to adopt good habits.

It may be useful to consider alternative input devices, such as a trackball, and, for some tasks, a microphone used with voice recognition software may be worth considering. Automatic data capture devices such as Optical Mark Recognition and Optical Character Recognition reduce the amount of data to be entered manually and may be a good investment if large quantities of similar data need to be entered. Touch screens are often used in busy situations such as call centres, but the position of the monitor needs to be considered very carefully if the user has to touch the screen as well as look at it.

Eye strain and headaches

There is no evidence that computer use causes disease or permanent damage to the eyes, but focusing on a screen for long periods of time can lead to tired eyes and headaches and this is likely to be made worse if the user feels under stress. It is important that the monitor is tilted and swivelled to the correct position for the user, and sited away from glare and reflection. Workers can ask their employers to provide and pay for an eyesight test, but the employer only needs to pay for spectacles if they are only needed for VDU work. Software design can also help to reduce eye strain, as explained later in this section.

End of sub-topic questions

1. A jewellery designer has decided to set up an online store to sell her clothing direct to the public. She has decided to employ an assistant who will be responsible for processing the customer orders, dealing with correspondence, ordering materials and other essential items. These jobs will involve the assistant using the computer for most of the day. List three features the designer should look for when buying the furniture and equipment for the computer workstation in order to protect the health of the assistant.

2. Once the equipment has been provided, the designer must make sure that the assistant is trained to look after his own health and safety. Describe three issues you would need to cover in such a training programme, explaining why each of them is important.

Activity

In groups, discuss the possible ways that employees working in a call centre could be made aware of the health and safety risks they face when using computers. Design a method of increasing awareness or produce training material that could be used as part of an induction programme for new staff members.

▶ 5.2 Health and safety of software

Software design

When they think about health and safety, most people tend to think about the workstation and hardware, but the way software is designed is also extremely important:

- The background and font colours used for the user interface should not cause strain to the user's eyes, with good contrast to make text stand out clearly. Ideally, the user should be able to adjust colours to suit their personal preferences. This can be particularly important for users who have any form of visual impairment.

- Font sizes need to be considered carefully. They should be large enough for the user to read easily, but not so large that the user has to scroll unnecessarily to see the whole screen. Again, the ability to adjust font size may be important for some users.

■ If menus are badly laid out, the user will have to move the mouse more to find the features required. Logical menu layout reduce the number of mouse clicks and also reduce the stress of the user who is not having to waste time hunting for the correct options.

■ Screen icons and other interactive controls should be laid out in logical groups fairly close together to avoid unnecessary mouse movement. Operations that require the user to work with depressed finger buttons (such as scrolling and dragging should be kept to a minimum).

■ Keyboard shortcuts can be a useful alternative to icons and menus, because they allow the user to choose their preferred method. This can reduce stress and allow the user to alternate their movements between keyboard and mouse, thus spreading the load on the joints. Users should be encouraged to vary the method they use to point to, select and manipulate objects.

■ Macros, either built into the software or defined by the user, can perform complex sequences of actions with a single key press or mouse click. This can reduce the number of key presses or mouse clicks the user needs to perform.

■ Software should be designed to accept input from a wide variety of devices, including voice input, touch screens and a variety of automatic data capture devices such as OCR and bar-code readers.

■ A help option should be provided to reduce stress for novice users.

End of sub-topic questions

3 You have been asked to design a database management system for a small farm business that delivers organic vegetables direct to the door of the customer. Orders are taken by telephone and the system calculates monthly bills for each customer, depending on what they have ordered. Describe how you would use the features of the software to help to protect the health and safety of the data-entry operator.

Stress

Whilst most workers experience stress to some extent, there are some features of computer-based work that can make stress more likely. Call centres and data-entry centres often monitor their staff very closely, and the nature of the work means that it is extremely easy to check up on work rates. Operators are sometimes expected to process transactions very quickly, and this can create a great deal of stress. It is important that targets set for operators are reasonable and build in breaks or changes of activity to reduce the impact on health and safety. Under these conditions, it is extremely important that when the software is designed, the user's health is taken into consideration. Stress levels for operators are likely to rise considerably if they feel they have to use inefficient menu structures or if the response time to a request for information is too long. Stress is likely to increase the chances of the operators suffering from headaches and other aches and pains.

Did you know?

There are a variety of programs designed to help you use your computer safely. Some applications remind the user to take a break, or show the user how to stretch and exercise to reduce the chances of injury. Training in ergonomics, risk assessment and other aspects of health and safety can also be provided on computer.

☑ *In this section you have covered:*

- the Health and Safety at Work Act, Display Screen Equipment Regulations
- risk assessment and the way it can be used to identify hazards that users may be exposed to and build in precautions to reduce the risk of damage to health
- the Display Screen Equipment Regulations that are designed to keep computer users safe
- the risks and hazards that may apply to computer use:
  - back pain and spinal damage caused by sitting in one position for a long time, often with poor posture
  - eye strain and headaches caused by focusing on the screen for long periods, particularly if the user interface screen is badly designed
  - upper limb disorders and damage to joints caused by repeated movements of the same joints, which can be made worse by inefficient software controls
- the precautions that can be taken to reduce the risks:
  - well-designed workstations with adjustable chairs and other furniture
  - screens that tilt and swivel so that their height can be adjusted
  - well-designed software layouts
  - varying input methods and software designed to reduce the number of key presses and mouse clicks
  - regular breaks or changes of activity
  - staff training to make users aware of the hazards and how to minimise them by working safely
  - the employer has a responsibility to provide safe equipment such as adjustable furniture, and to train the employees to look after their own health and safety, for example by teaching them to adjust their chair to the correct position. It is then the responsibility of the employees to follow that advice and use the equipment safely. Anyone whose health is damaged because they chose to ignore the advice then has no claim upon their employer.

6 Analysis and design

In this section you will cover:

- how to identify the problem a client has

- how to write a design specification

- how to document the input, processing and output that takes place

- documenting a solution design

- designing to reduce data-entry errors.

Key terms

Client: the person who needs the solution to a problem.

End-user: the person who will actually use the solution.

Audience: the person or people who the final product could be aimed at.

In this section you will learn to design and produce ICT-based solutions to problems.

Analysing a problem can seem difficult, and it's a skill that certainly needs to be practised. It's important to find out exactly what the client needs, and it takes skill to find that out without using technical language the client may not understand. Once you know what the solution needs to do, documenting it will help you produce good designs, and a good analysis will also help you evaluate how successful your solution is.

A system design should be documented clearly enough for another person to use your design sheets to build the solution. Designs will often change as you find problems or think of new ideas, but having a clear idea of what you intend to do before you start makes implementation much easier.

6.1 Analysis of problems

Identifying problems

Analysing a problem is the first step towards creating a solution for it. The problem should not be one for yourself, it should be for someone else. The person who needs the solution to a problem is your **client**. When defining the problem and finding a solution you will need to consider carefully the person who will actually use the solution, the **end-user**, and the person or people who the final product could be aimed at, the **audience**.

Worked example

> MicroPhones need to find ways to attract business to their new mobile phone shop. Shaun Coppell, their marketing manager, needs to be able to produce effective advertising material to give to potential customers. He is considering employing an ICT expert to build a MicroPhones website.
>
> - MicroPhones is the client.
> - Shaun is the end-user.
> - The customers are the audience.

Identifying user/client requirements

The most important part of producing a requirements specification is understanding the problem your client has. There are several ways you can find out more about the problem:

- Interview the client.
- Use a questionnaire to collect information/data.
- Look at existing paperwork.
- Observe your client/end-user.

Interview

The most obvious way of finding out what your client needs is to ask them in person by carrying out an interview. It is important to prepare carefully for the interview by:

Fig. 6.1 *Different marketing methods*

- arranging an appointment
- preparing your questions in advance
- having a way of recording what the client says – usually by writing things down, but if the client doesn't mind, you might find it useful to record what was said.

Questionnaire

Questionnaires can feel a bit impersonal, but they can be an effective way of getting the views of a number of people. If you have several end users, a questionnaire might be a good way of finding out what they want. Using closed questions makes the answers easier to analyse. If you ask the question 'How often do you use your computer?', you could get a whole variety of answers from 'Lots' to 'One hour a day', to 'Every day'. It is much better to give a choice of answers. A better question would be:

Q1. Do you use your computer?

Less than 1 hour a day ☐

1–4 hours a day ☐

More than 4 hours a day ☐

The limited choice of answers makes it easy to analyse.

The definite times makes it easier for the user to decide which answer is correct.

The tick boxes make it quick to fill in.

> **Activity**
>
> Prepare a set of questions for an initial interview with Shaun Coppell.

> **Remember**
>
> Your client may not have much technical knowledge. Avoid using jargon and phrase your questions simply and clearly.

> **Activity**
>
> Design a questionnaire you could use to find out what MicroPhones' employees think of their current advertising methods and material. If you are going to improve the material, you need to know what aspects of it they like and dislike and find out how they think customers react to it. You might also want to use new methods, and this would be an opportunity to test your ideas. Because a lot of this is opinion rather than fact, you need to think of how to code these **value judgements**.

> **Key terms**
>
> **Value judgement:** judgement or opinion rather than a fact.

◤ Existing paperwork

Finding out what paperwork is currently used is a good way of understanding what is going on. It can help you to work out what the inputs and outputs of the solution will need to be. Using a document record sheet (see microsite for example) is a good way of writing down what you find out from each document.

A document might show you:

■ what data is used in the system
■ what format the data takes
■ what the output document needs to look like.

■ Did you know?

If an organisation has British Standards approval, the format of their important documents will have been inspected. It may be important to your client that the format of the document doesn't change, because if it does, they would have to get it approved again.

■ Activity

A customer enquiry slip would be used for the staff at MicroPhones to note down what a customer wants. Look at the slip on the microsite and fill in a document record sheet for it. Don't worry if you can't fill in every piece of information – that's often the case. Sometimes the information won't apply, sometimes you would need to ask the end user about it.

◤ Observation

Sometimes it is useful to watch what is going on in an organisation. Looking at people working in the situation can help you to see where the problems occur.

You should always ask permission before you observe people working. Try to get an idea of:

■ what programs people are using
■ whether they seem physically comfortable
■ whether they seem stressed
■ how much time they spend waiting for their system to respond.

You probably won't use all of these methods – just pick the ones that fit the situation best.

■ End of sub-topic questions

1. Finding out what users think about their current software solution is important. Suggest appropriate techniques for each of the following situations and justify your answer:

   a a 24-hour call centre with 100 operators who work shifts

   b a management consultancy business run by one person.

2. Choose a document generated by your school or college. Fill in a document record sheet for it. Make a list of questions you would need to ask to enable you to complete the form.

■ Writing a requirements specification

Now comes what many people find the trickiest bit of the whole process, and one of the most important. You need to look carefully at the information you have and use it to write a list that says *exactly what the solution to the problem must do*.

Limits

Sometimes a client might explain a very large and complex problem. If that happens, you need to break it down into smaller ones and decide which one you are going to tackle. It is better to solve a smaller problem well than a large one badly.

Detail

Data capture:

- Where will the data come from?
- What type of data will it be?
- In what format?
- How much data will there be?
- How often will new data occur?

Function – what the system actually has to do:

- Produce an invoice.

Function – how it will do it – the processes:

- What calculations need to be done?
- What sorts and searches will be needed?
- How will the user navigate the system?
- Will the system need to be interactive?

User interface:

- The **user interface** involves choosing suitable input and output devices and designing screen layouts that are appropriate to the person using them.
- Who will be using the system?
- How much computer skill do they have?
- Do they have any special needs, such as difficulty with seeing or moving the screen pointer accurately?
- How long will they be using the system for?
- What input and output devices are available?
- Does the system need to reflect a **house style?**

Output:

- What documents will the system need to produce?
- Will they need to be electronic, on paper or both?
- Will the system need to produce sounds? If so, will just the end user hear them or everyone in the room?
- Will they only be used within the organisation, or by customers or other people outside it?

Storage:

- What data will need to be stored?
- How long will it need to be stored for?
- Will any special files names need to be used?
- What directory structure will be used?
- If files are to be stored on a web server, will they have to follow any special rules?

> ### Key terms
>
> **User interface:** involves the aspects of the system that a person interacts with to use and control the system; involves input and output devices as well as screen layouts.
>
> **House style:** used by some organisations to make all the documents and interfaces look consistent; might involve colours, the use of a logo, font sizes and styles.

Fig. **6.2** *Your interface must be designed with the end user's needs in mind*

Key terms

Access rights: allow users to do different things. A file might be marked 'read only', so that only users with the password can change it. In a big system, different parts might have different access rights.

Remember

If any personal data is stored on the system, the Data Protection Act will usually apply.

Security:

■ Is any of the data in the system confidential?

■ Will all users have the same **access rights**?

■ Do some parts of the system need to be hidden from the user in case they get deleted or damaged?

Writing the requirements specification

Your requirements specification can be written as a list. Each point should be made clearly on a new line. You could use a bulleted list if you want to.

Sometimes it is useful to draw a diagram to describe what is happening.

End of sub-topic questions

3 Which features of this book show the use of Nelson Thornes' house style?

4 Draw a diagram that shows what happens when a new customer enters the shop and enquires about phones as described earlier in this section.

Activity

Write a specification for the problems that MicroPhones have when a new customer arrives in the shop and wants to know which phones and tariffs would suit them best.

or

MicroPhones have also said that they wish to improve their methods of getting information to customers who have filled in an enquiry form. Write a specification that would cover this problem.

You may not have all the information you need to build a full specification. Make a list of the questions you would need to ask Shaun at MicroPhones to complete the specification you have written.

Approving the user requirements

When you have written a list of the requirements, it is important to go back to the client and check it. You need to make sure you have understood all the requirements correctly and that nothing has been missed out.

Identifying input, processing and output

Think about each stage in the process and:

Decide what information needs to be produced as an output.

List the data that will need to be put into the system.

Work out what processing the computer will need to do to turn the input into the output.

Talking photo album

Problem identification:

Arun attended his sister's wedding recently. He took photographs with his digital camera and asked guests to wish the happy couple good luck either by typing a message or recording one by speaking into a microphone. He has some great pictures and sound bites, although some of them need to be edited to improve their quality. He wants to put together a talking photo album that he can send copies of to family and friends.

Arun is the user, his sister is the client and their family and friends are the audience for this solution.

The client's requirements include:

- A photograph album containing:
    - digital photos from the wedding
    - messages from the wedding guests
- which can be electronically copied and sent to friends.

Input	Processing	Output
Pictures from digital camera	Crop, remove red eye, adjust brightness and contrast, resize and compress	Usable photographs at correct size for pages and small file size
Sound recordings from microphone in wav format	Remove background noise, adjust volume, cut to reduce any that are too long. Compress to MP3 format	Short, clear sound bites with low file size
Typed good luck messages	Edit if necessary	Short messages in guests' own words
	Arrange photographs on pages and add captions and written messages. Decorate using background, picture frames, clip art. Set up hyperlinks to play sound files	Attractive pages that show pictures and text and play appropriate sound bites when hyperlinks are clicked
	Set up navigation using hyperlinks so that the user can move around interactively rather than having to follow a set path	Interactive multimedia album that can be copied and sent to relatives and friends

College enrolment system

Problem identification:

Imagine a new student is joining a college. The college has course details stored in a database. The student fills in an application form with their personal details and chosen course, which are entered into the database. The student is given printed details of their course and its lecturers. Lecturers are given lists of students taking each course.

Input	Processing	Output
Course details (e.g. department, subject, level, lecturer) entered into course table		Course record displayed on screen
Student personal details (e.g. name, contact details) stored in student table		Student record displayed on screen
Code of course preferred by student	Student added to course set list	Printed course details for student Set list e-mailed to lecturer

⬛ 6.2 Design of solutions

Selecting design tools and techniques

The tools and techniques you choose will of course depend on the problem. The important thing is to make sure that you have considered the alternatives you have available and choose the ones most suitable for the problem you want to solve. There may be more than one approach within the software you have chosen, and you will need to choose the most appropriate techniques. A standard letter, for instance, could be designed using a template or linked to a database via a mail merge. If a large number of letters are generated at once, a mail merge will probably be best. Letters sent to one or two people at a time might be better done through a template.

Input – design of data entry

Making sure that data is entered accurately and efficiently is very important. The design will need to take into account: what form the data takes (text, picture, sound, video, etc.), how much data there is, how often it is input and what devices are available.

Data capture devices

Automatic data capture devices such as bar-code readers can be useful when there is a lot of data to be entered as they are often quicker than manual data entry and may have built-in error checking. If they have to be bought specially, they add to the cost of the system, and so their advantages may need to be considered alongside the cost. Another example would be a webcam that automatically starts to record when movement is sensed, for example recording video for a video diary of an animal or bird.

Large quantities of manual data entry can also cause RSI in operators, and would be a reason for considering OCR or voice recognition software.

In many cases keying the data in manually may be the only practical choice, and in this case, other methods must be found to reduce data-entry errors as much as possible.

Validation

Validation is a method of checking data to try to reduce the number of errors in data being entered. It tests the data against the **validation rule** and gives the user an **error message** if the data does not pass the test. There are many different types of validation:

- A **presence check** is the simplest form of validation. It makes sure that some data has been entered.
- A **range check** checks that the data is within a certain range of letters or numbers. For example, a phone price has to be a number between £50 and £500; £70 would be allowed, but £35 would not.
- A **format check** checks data follows the correct pattern. For instance, a product code might have to be three letters followed by three digits; PAF741 would be accepted, but PAF74 would not.

AQA Examiner's tip

You will be expected to take some work on problem identification into the examination. This should include details of the problem, a list of the client's requirements and interpretation of those requirements as input, processing and output. A test plan and testing evidence will also be required for the examination. One problem can be addressed for the identification, and another can be addressed for the testing (or one problem can be used for both).

Key terms

Validation: computer-based check that the data being entered is reasonable. It tests the data against a **validation rule**, for example an exam mark may only be between 0 and 90. An error message is designed to tell the user they have made a mistake. It is best if they are clear about the error, for instance 'Please enter a number between 0 and 90' is clearer than 'Data out of range'.

Error message: tells the user they have made a mistake. It is best if they are clear about the error, for instance 'Please enter a number between 0 and 90' is clearer than 'Data out of range'.

	C	D	E	F	G	H
1	Form	Mod1/50	Mod 2/50	Mod 3/50	Average	Effort Grade
2	12P	12	30	37	26	A
3	12N	26	33	36	32	G
4	12N	20	14	32	22	D
5	12P	20	27	34	27	A
6	12P	27	27			A
7	12N	16	34			B
8	12P	22	26			A
9	12N	6	24	15	15	D
10	12P	12	36	53	34	C
11	12N	29	35	59	41	A
12	12P	0	26	28	18	B
13	12N	12	21	59	31	A
14	12P	5	18	4	9	B

Incorrect Grade

⊗ Please enter a grade of A,B,C,D or E

Retry   Cancel

Fig. 6.3 *Clear error messages guide the user regarding the form of input that is required*

AQA Examiner's tip

Most questions about validation ask you to give an example, and many candidates forget to do so. Sometimes the example needs to be chosen from information given in the question. If the question has multiple parts, make sure you don't use the same validation technique twice.

■ A **length check** makes sure that the correct number of characters has been entered.

■ A **list** or **look up check** makes sure that the data is on a list of acceptable values.

■ A **cross field check** makes sure that two fields are always entered correctly each time they are entered into a record. For instance, if a certain phone contract is only available on one network, it will be rejected if a different network is entered.

■ A **check digit** is used to make sure long numbers, such as those generated by bar codes, are entered correctly. A complex calculation is carried out using the digits in the number, and the check digit is the result of those calculations. In an EPOS system, the scanner would usually show a red light and make a beeping noise if the check digit does not match.

Verification

Validation should reduce data-entry errors, but it cannot remove them completely. If a MicroPhones customer's date of birth was entered as 06/05/02 instead of 06/08/52, it might still be valid, but the system would reject the customer for a contract phone because they are too young. One way to avoid this would be to check the data by proofreading it against the application form filled in by the customer. This is known as **verification**, and is a good way of avoiding transcription errors, errors made by the user not entering the data exactly as it was written on the form.

Key terms

Verification: a check to make sure data has not been corrupted as it is copied between different parts of a computer system or entered from a source document.

Data capture forms

Data is often recorded by filling in a data capture form. Sometimes these are paper based, like the MicroPhones customer enquiry form shown in Fig. 6.2, sometimes the data is entered directly into the computer. You

Fig. 6.4 *Transcription errors can happen when data is entered manually*

may have to decide which of the two methods is better in the situation you are designing for.

Computer-based forms can have built-in validation, and can be quicker than writing out the data and then entering it manually. That also means that the person has to have a computer available when they need to enter data, so in the case of MicroPhones, each member of the sales team would need a computer workstation.

Paper-based forms can be filled in anywhere and entered into the computer at a convenient time, perhaps by a data-entry operator rather than the employee who filled them in. There can be problems if the data hasn't been written clearly or has been written into the wrong part of the form or in the wrong format.

If the data from a paper-based form is going to be transferred to a computer-based form, it is useful if both forms have a similar layout, as the person entering the data is less likely to make data-entry errors.

Specialist data-entry forms are needed for data-entry methods such as OMR and OCR. The forms then need to be scanned and interpreted by specialist software.

Designing a computer-based data-entry form

Fig. 6.5 Paper-based and computer-based forms

Things to think about

- Make it obvious where data needs to be entered, perhaps by using boxes or by the use of colour.
- Give the user some idea of how much data you are expecting by varying the size of the box appropriately.
- Where a limited number of choices are available use features like drop-down boxes, tick boxes or radio buttons.
- On a form you can often control the way the user moves through the fields, so think about the order in which you expect the data to be entered.
- Build in validation so that the chances of the data being entered wrongly are reduced.
- E-mail addresses and passwords may need to be entered twice for verification.

Designing user interfaces

If you have made a good job of analysing the problem, your specification should tell you a lot about what the user interface should be like.

Things to think about

- What input and output devices will be used? These may not be traditional devices such as monitors and keyboards, but could involve mobile phones, MP3 players or video cameras.
- What will the screen display look like? How much screen area will the user have available? Will pictures display properly or is a text-only version necessary? Visually impaired people may need voice output to read out text and describe graphics.
- What colours will be used? Think about house style and colours that are clear for the user.

■ The interface should feel intuitive to the user. The navigation should seem logical. The number of key presses or mouse clicks needed should be kept to a minimum.

■ Processing design

■ **PC activity**

Use the planning documents found at www.nelsonthones.com/aqaqce/ict_resource.htm to help you design the process.

Your design should include details of processing to be carried out such as calculations, sorts and searches to convert the data into information. The way you design the processing of the solution will depend on the type of software you are going to use. The important thing is to plan the solution logically and document how you expect it to work. When you build your solution, you may find that you need to change your designs. That isn't a problem; you just need to make sure that you document the things you changed and the reason you changed them.

Examples of design procedures are:

Spreadsheet

Using blank spreadsheet grids, you should show:

■ the name and function of each worksheet you will use

■ what cells will be used for storing the data and displaying the information

■ how the cells will be formatted

■ the functions and formulae that will be used

■ which cells and worksheets will be protected for security.

You will also need to show:

■ what macros will be needed and the function of each one

■ how the worksheets will be linked and how users will navigate between them.

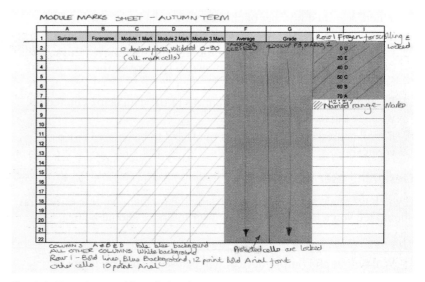

Fig. 6.6 *Example spreadsheet design sheet*

Database management systems

You need to think about:

■ what fields will be needed in each database table

■ whether the database needs to be relational, and what tables need to be linked

■ data types, formats and validation for each field
■ what queries will be needed
■ what forms and reports are required and how they will be laid out
■ how the user will navigate the database management systems.

Database File	Cottage Rentals	Table Name	tblCottage	(Composite) Key Field	Cottage ID		
Related to							
Table Name		*Foreign Key*		*Table Name*		*Foreign Key*	
Rental		Cottage ID					

General Table Description: List of cottages for rent

Field Name	R	I	Data type	Length	Input Mask/Validation	Default Value	Description	Typical Data
Cottage ID	Y	Y	Autonumber				Unique ID	49
Name of Cottage	Y	Y	Text	30				Holly Cottage
No of bedrooms	Y		Number	2 digits	whole number between 1 and 6			2
Max Occupancy	Y		Number	2 digits	whole number between 2 and 15		No of people allowed	
Area	Y		Text	3 Digits	PEM or DER or SCO or NOR		Pembrokeshire, Derbyshire, Scotland, Norfolk	PEM
Nearest town			Text	25				Matlock
Linen Supplied			Yes/No	3	Yes or No	Yes		

Fig. 6.7 *Example of a table design sheet*

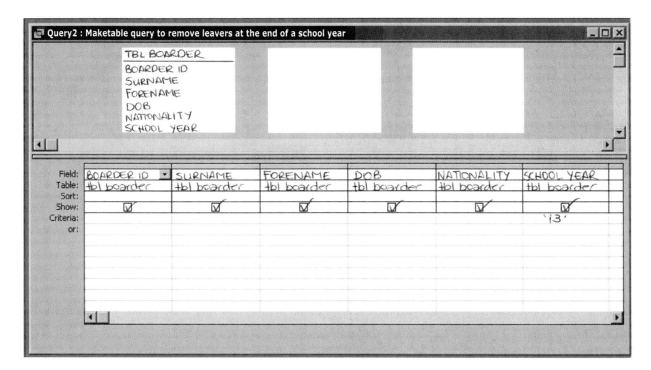

Fig. 6.8 *Example of a query design sheet for a maketable query*

💻 PC activity

Design a database management system for MicroPhones' staff that will allow them to enter customer enquiries to be stored in a database. Design queries that will allow staff to:

1 call up a customer's details when their surname is entered

2 search for the name and address of all customers on a particular tariff so that MicroPhones can e-mail special offers they may find attractive.

■ Remember

It's best to control the size of graphics for webpages by pixels rather than centimetres to reduce the effects of different screen resolutions.

■ Remember

The specification states that the designs you produce should be clear enough to allow a third party to build your solution using them. That means that you don't have to explain how to set up each feature, but you do have to say how each feature would be used. For example, you would not need to explain what a lookup function does or how to set one up, but you do have to explain which value is being looked up in which table and what column holds the value to be returned.

Webpages or interactive presentations

You will need to show:

- which items are on your main template and so appear on every page in the same place
- the file name and size of all items on the page
- the keywords that belong to each webpage
- a file structure to show how all the files are stored and what file size they are
- how the interactivity works – what the user will do to make things happen
- any effects you are using, such as rollovers and colour changes
- details of any animated objects, such as the path they appear from and how long they play for
- details of sound effects – how long they play for, whether they can be switched off
- any transitions or build effects.

💻 PC activity

Design a home page for an intranet webpage for MicroPhones' staff that will allow them to find details of handsets and tariffs and enter customer enquiries to be stored in a database.

■ Output design

The user interface will include screen-based, paper-based and sound outputs. Remember that the user may not use the same screen settings as you did, and so the interface should be tested on the equipment they will be using if possible. If the solution is a webpage, it may not be possible to take into account every screen the user might use to view it, but it is important to allow for smaller screens when you design your pages. The screen design should try to minimise the number of key presses and mouse clicks the user has to make, so drop-down lists and radio buttons should be used where a user has to choose between options, for instance.

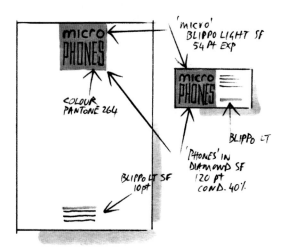

Fig. 6.9 *Hand-drawn document design for paper-based outputs*

If your output involves sound, it may be advisable for the user to be able to switch it off if they are working in a public place or just find it irritating.

Printed output may need to fit in with a house style or follow a particular pattern if it is part of the client's paperwork for British Standards approval. Many documents will need to be photocopied, so designs that work well in black and white as well as colour may be preferred. The media that the output needs to be printed on is important too, as is the printer that is going to be used. Some types of graphics, particularly photographs, may not print well on laser printers, and this may govern the type of artwork to be used.

For more on input, processing and output, see Section 9.

Training

When the final solution has been designed, it should be possible to decide what training the client and end users will need. The client will have to allow time for people to be trained to use it, and training materials will be needed too. These could be electronic or paper-based.

 Activity

You have decided that the best solution for Shaun Coppell of MicroPhones is to set up a web-based database management system for all staff to enter customer enquiries. He now needs training materials to teach his staff to use the new database and to give them some support once the system is in place. Discuss the various ways these materials could be provided and the advantages and disadvantages of each method.

Test planning

An important stage of the design of the system will be planning how to test that it works effectively. This will be covered in Section 7 in more detail.

Client approval

It is important to make sure that the client is happy with the designs before the system is built. The end users may also need to see the designs at this stage. It is important that the designs are clear enough for the client to understand. It may be useful to set up user interface screens so that the client and end user can see how they would look and make comments on them. They do not have to work at this stage, but it may be easier to decide whether they would be appropriate if they are screen- rather than paper-based.

✓ *In this section you have covered:*

- identifying problems suitable for ICT solutions
- the difference between a client, an end user and an audience
- the methods available for investigating a client's problem
- the information that needs to be included in a specification
- using diagrams to help explain a problem
- identifying input, output and processing needs
- designing data-entry forms and user interfaces
- minimising data-entry errors through validation
- documenting process designs
- designing output formats
- planning user training
- obtaining client approval.

7 Implementation and testing

In this section you will cover:

- planning for implementation
- documenting implementation
- producing a test strategy and plan
- documenting the results of testing.

Having drawn up detailed design plans for the task you are undertaking, you now need to implement the designs to produce a working solution within the timescale you have available. Part of that process will be to test the solution to make sure that it is suitable for your client and does the job that is required of it.

7.1 Planning for implementation

Identifying sub-tasks

The first thing that you need to do is to break the overall tasks down into smaller sections, sometimes called sub-tasks. This helps to identify exactly what needs to be done within the time that is available.

Time planning

Having looked at the list of sub-tasks, it is important to make sure that they can all be fitted into the time you have available. You need to think about:

- how long each task will take
- in what order the tasks need to be done – some tasks may not be possible until a previous one has been completed
- whether any tasks have to be done at a specific time – usually these are tasks that involve other people and it is particularly important to plan these in advance, rather than just assume that other people will work around your needs.

Some tasks may overlap, for example if you hand out questionnaires to collect input data, you can work on building the spreadsheet to analyse the results whilst waiting for the responses.

It is important to be realistic about the time each task will take and allow extra time in case things go wrong.

The time plan could be recorded in any way that suits you. Some people like to use a simple calendar, entering what job needs to be done on each day. The calendar could be paper-based or electronic, perhaps even using the reminder system built in to many mobile phones. Other people like to use a **Gantt chart** to block in the time for each task. One advantage of a Gantt chart is that it is easier to show overlapping tasks than it is on a calendar.

Building a time plan can be strangely satisfying. All the tasks are there, it looks beautifully neat, organised and efficient. It is also completely useless unless it is used as a working document. It is inevitable that the plan will change, because some tasks may take less time than anticipated, and it is almost certain that some will take more. If this happens, the time plan may need to be revised to make sure the final schedule can be met.

Key terms

Gantt chart: a time-based grid that shows tasks and resources to accomplish a job.

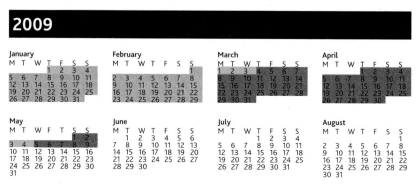

Jan					Feb				Mar	
Week										
1	2	3	4	5	6	7	8	9	10	11
	End User Testing									
	Implementation and alpha testing									
	Modification post user testing									

Fig. 7.1 *Gantt charts make it easy to show overlapping tasks*

2009

January	February	March	April
M T W T F S S	M T W T F S S	M T W T F S S	M T W T F S S

Fig. 7.2 *Time plan using an ordinary calendar*

Worked example

You are making a blog for the school drama department to use as part of their marketing material. It is based on a 'behind the scenes' look at producing a play, showing the preparations for it and how the people involved feel about what they are doing. It will involve interviews, still photographs and short video clips with text-based material to link the sections together. The final result will be displayed on the school intranet to encourage people to think about taking Drama for A Level, AS Level. The designs have been discussed and agreed with your client, the head of Drama.

You would need to:

- Obtain permission from the people you want to record. Some people may not be prepared to appear in interviews. You may need parental permission to use images of students.

- Make a list of people you want to photograph or interview, and make appointments to do so.

- Make a note of the dates of any rehearsals you wish to photograph or record.

- Edit the photographs, sound and video clips.

- Get approval for the clips you want to use.

- Build the pages that form the background for the other material.

- Set up the navigation between pages.

- Link the media files to the correct places in the blog.

- Create thumbnails for any files where the user has a choice about whether to view.

- Test the system.
- Get approval for the finished product.
- Upload it to the intranet.

Some of the dates involved, such as rehearsals or performances, may be fixed, so those would need to be built into the time plan first.

Dates to record other sections need to be arranged in advance with the people concerned, so they would need to be agreed and entered next.

The other jobs can then be fitted into the time frame, allowing some extra time for emergencies, so that the final deadline is met.

Implementing a solution

The exact process you will go through when implementing your solution will obviously vary enormously, depending on the task you are attempting, but there are certain general rules that apply in most situations.

Follow your time plan

Having gone to the trouble of making a plan, you should stick to it as far as you can. You may have to make changes, in which case the plan needs to be updated to make sure you keep on schedule.

Follow your design plans

It is inevitable that the solution you are building will change and develop as you go along, and your original design ideas may need to be modified, but they should provide a good starting point. If you make changes to the design, keep a note of what they are and what the reason was.

Document what you do

You do not have to take evidence of your implementation into the examination with you, but it is useful to keep a log of your progress through the task, and that will be useful information for any future work you do. Taking regular screen dumps and making brief notes to accompany them is a good way of documenting your progress, and they can be saved with a name that includes the date. This also gives you a useful record if you need to go back and change anything at a later date. You will need to take evidence of testing that you have carried out into the examination with you.

Did you know?

A project like the one outlined above is straightforward if the material has been written by the students themselves. If the play involves copyright material, the copyright holder would have to give their permission for any recorded material you wish to use. Many of them do not allow their shows to be recorded at all, so you would need to check this out before beginning the project.

Did you know?

Prototyping is a method of developing a solution that involves building a small section, testing it and improving it, then adding the next part so that the solution is developed in stages rather than completely built from pre-existing designs.

End of sub-topic questions

1. You have been asked to produce a newsletter about your school or college's last set of external examination results to be used as marketing material at an open day for prospective Year 7 students. Make a list of sub-tasks you will need to carry out for this project.

2. Why is it important to make a time plan before commencing a project? Using the example above or an example project of your choice, draw up a time plan that is as realistic as you can make it using a Gantt chart and another using a calendar. Which of the two methods do you find more useful? Why?

■ 7.2 Test planning

It is obviously important to make sure that the solution you produce works, and that it meets the requirements of your client. A test strategy and test plan should be drawn up when your solution is being designed so that as you implement each aspect of the solution you can carry out the appropriate tests to make sure it works. The complete solution can then be tested to make sure all of the sections work together to ensure that it does its job to the satisfaction of the client.

Test strategy

Producing a test strategy is a useful way of planning what testing you need to carry out. It looks at each aspect of the solution that needs to be tested and outlines how the process will be carried out. For instance, if the solution involved a spreadsheet with validated cells, the test strategy would specify the proportion of the cells to be tested and the type of test data that will be used.

Test data

When designing a test procedure, it is very important to specify what data is going to be used in the tests. There are three types of test data: **normal**, **boundary** and **erroneous**.

Worked example

A field in a database is designed to accept examination marks. The marks are always whole numbers, and the maximum mark available is 90. Validation has been set up to accept:

■ numbers

■ without decimals

■ within the range 0 to 90.

Each aspect of that validation needs to be tested.

Normal data should not break any of the rules, so a value of 63 would be an example of normal data that should be accepted by the field.

Values of 0 and 90 would be boundary and normal data and should also be accepted.

A value of 91 is just outside the boundary and erroneous and so should be rejected.

Any text value should be rejected, so a value of 'Smith' should bring up a validation message to warn the user that the data is invalid.

Similarly, a number with a decimal should fail validation, so 43.6 should not be accepted.

■ Test plan

It is sometimes said that the purpose of testing is to make the system fail. It should try to find any weak points in the system that might make the solution difficult to use or even stop it working.

■ Key terms

Normal data: the type of data that will be entered most of the time. It should be accepted by the system and should give the expected result when processed.

Boundary data: data that tests the inside and outside limits of what should be accepted and rejected.

Erroneous data: data that is inappropriate. If possible, validation checks should reject this kind of data, but if this is not possible, it is important that the system can continue to operate.

The test plan should aim to prove:

- the validity of data input
- the accuracy of output
- the presentation of output
- that the solution meets the requirements of the client
- that the solution is usable by the end user and/or intended audience.

It should incorporate the data to be used for testing the solution and the expected results of each test.

Validation

The information produced by any system is only as reliable as the data entered into it. Remember, GIGO (garbage in, garbage out). If the data entered into the system is incorrect, perhaps because of **transcription errors** caused by the data not being copied correctly from the source document, then the information will be wrong as a result. This can be dangerous, as the information may not show any obvious signs of being wrong. Whilst it is impossible for any system to completely prevent incorrect data being entered, validation checks can reduce the likelihood of it happening.

Where validation checks are in place, it is important to make sure that they are doing their job in allowing normal data through and rejecting data that is erroneous, bringing up appropriate error messages where possible.

The nature of some tasks may mean that there is a great deal of validation that is extremely similar, and in this case it is not necessary to test and document every example. If a system processes examination marks for hundreds of students and all the marks follow the same rules, it is enough to test a few examples from that field to make sure that the rule is operating correctly.

Using a database management system, for example:

- Presence checks should be tested to make sure that the user cannot move on to the next record until a value has been entered in the required field.
- Format checks should test that only data of the correct pattern is accepted. For instance, if the field should accept two letters followed by three numbers, it should accept FG476 but reject FGK76 or F6476.
- Range checks should be tested to make sure that only data within the range is accepted (see example above).
- Length checks may ensure only an exact number of characters or a maximum number of characters is accepted.
- Lookup checks should ensure that the value being entered corresponds to a record stored elsewhere. For instance, a student candidate number should belong to a student whose details are stored in the system. Check boxes and drop-down lists are often used to make sure the user can only select values that are valid.
- When planning the testing for any validated field, the test data should be specified and the appropriate error message should be described.
- The test plan for the example described above might look like this:

Key terms

Transcription errors: can occur when data is being transferred manually, usually from a paper-based document. For example, an examination mark written on the sheet as 87 might be entered as 57, perhaps because the number 8 was not written clearly enough.

AQA Examiner's tip

Don't test inbuilt functions of the applications software, e.g. Autonumber, and avoid repetitive tests of navigation functions such as buttons to turn pages.

Table 7.1 *Validation test plan*

Test number	Test	Data type	Data value	Expected outcome
1	Exam Mark field validation	Normal	63	Data Accepted
2		Boundary	0	Data Accepted
3		Boundary	90	Data Accepted
4		Erroneous (fraction)	43.6	Error Message 'Please enter a whole number between 0 and 90'
5		Erroneous (Text)	Smith	Error Message 'Please enter a whole number between 0 and 90'
6		Erroneous	99	Error Message 'Please enter a whole number between 0 and 90'
7		Boundary	91	Error Message 'Please enter a whole number between 0 and 90'

Accuracy of output

The reason for producing a computer-based solution to a problem is to produce accurate output, and to do this, the processing carried out must be set up correctly. The processing will naturally vary depending on the task being carried out, but some examples might be:

■ A spreadsheet formula should produce the correct answer for the data that has been entered.

■ A database should return the correct results for the query that has been set up.

■ A website should display the correct page when a hyperlink is clicked.

■ The correct sound should play when the theatre operator presses the button to call up a sound effect.

■ The wedding photographs should appear in the correct order on the slide show.

■ A macro should carry out the required series of events without displaying an error message.

The test plan should identify each process that is being carried out, but, as explained above, it is not necessary to document the results of lots of identical tests. In this case it is sufficient to document a representative sample of the tests you have carried out.

It is also important to document the data being used, again using normal, boundary and erroneous data to make sure the results are correct and the solution continues to work.

Presentation of output

As far as the user is concerned, how the output is presented is extremely important, and it is an area that is often not tested enough by designers. User interfaces need to make it as easy as possible for the end user to use the solution, and their health and safety needs to be considered too.

On-screen forms need to be tested with data sets that mimic the process the user will go through, making sure data is displayed properly and that the user can move through each field on the form quickly and in a logical order. The text should be clear to read, and it should be easy to tell which sections of the form require data to be entered. Scrolling should be kept to a minimum.

Printed output needs to be clear and easy to read, with the information appearing in the correct place. Avoiding dense blocks of colour will reduce printing costs. It may be necessary to compare the printout to other documents to check that house style is being maintained.

If large numbers are generated as a result of a calculation, it is important that they are displayed correctly and this may not happen if the display space is too small. A cell full of hash characters may just mean that a spreadsheet column is too narrow, but it will confuse an inexperienced user.

A very common mistake when checking the presentation of output is to not include sufficient data. A report may print perfectly well when there are only a few records in the system, but not deal with large quantities nearly so well. If the report prints on more than one page, it may be necessary to check that headings are repeated and that groups of records stay together on the same page. Page numbers will help the user keep the pages in order. Whilst it is not advisable to waste time entering vast quantities of data, the test plan should include a data set that ensures that the solution can cope under such circumstances.

Whenever possible, the output should be tested on the hardware that the end user has available. A document may print very quickly and clearly on a top-of-the-range laser printer but take a long time and look blurred on an old inkjet. A webpage designed to display well on a large, high-resolution monitor may mean that users with older equipment may have to scroll so much that the site becomes unusable. It is obviously impossible to test a webpage on every type of monitor available, but some web design packages have built-in facilities to analyse how well webpages display in different browsers and on different hardware. Any output designed to appear on a portable device such as a laptop, PDA or mobile phone needs to be tested on a screen set to the appropriate size and settings.

It is important to try to test the system under its most demanding circumstances; for example, if an interactive multimedia presentation is playing a video, and the user clicks on the thumbnail to load a large image, will the system freeze, stop playing the video, load the picture in a different window or do nothing until the video has finished? Will the user know what is happening?

The appearance of the output is something that it is important to get the end user to test. Something that seems logical and intuitive to you may not seem so to a person who does not know how the system works, and their opinion of the end-user interface is extremely important.

Client requirements

The client is the person who needs a solution to a problem, and so it is obviously important that the client feels that the solution meets their requirements. The client's main concern is likely to be that the output provides accurate information in usable form, but their exact needs will vary depending on the task being attempted. These should have been defined in the specification, and should be built into the test plan. Their testing may take the form of a questionnaire or interview.

> **Remember**
>
> Documents often need to be photocopied, and many users do not have colour printing facilities. It is good practice to make sure that documents remain usable when printed in black and white.

> **Remember**
>
> The exception to the rule about proving that tests work is the testing of navigation macros that move from one page to another. These should obviously be tested, but there is no real evidence that can show that they work, so it is best to explain this as part of the test strategy rather than document a long list of tests with no evidence.

End-user requirements

The client may not be the person who will actually use the solution, and so it is also important that the end user's requirements are met. The end user is likely to be concerned with how easy the solution is to use, how long it takes to input data and produce the required output. The interface will be important to them, and it is their health and safety that can be protected by a good design. The end-user should test the system by using it, perhaps following a user guide. It can be useful to ask the user to follow instructions to input a specific set of data, designed to check the usability of all aspects of the solution, but it is also important to allow them to work through the solution in a way that feels logical to them, as this may bring up situations that have not been tested before.

Audience requirements

Some solutions will be prepared for an audience other than the client or end user. It may be possible to ask the client to arrange to show the material to suitable people, or you may have to arrange this for yourself. If you do this, it is important to choose people who are representative of the target audience. If an advertising leaflet is aimed at home buyers, testing it on a group of teenagers is unlikely to produce valid results. This testing is probably best carried out using a questionnaire that targets specific points such as the font sizes, readability and information included. As these are value judgements, you need to decide how they can best be coded so that you can analyse them usefully.

Testing

As the solution is built, the test plan should be followed and the results recorded. The best way to do this is to use a modified version of the test plan that records the actual outcome and any corrective action needed as a result of failed tests.

Table 7.2 *Validation testing*

Test number	Test	Data value	Expected outcome	Actual outcome
1	Exam Mark field validation	63	Data Accepted	Data accepted
2		0	Data Accepted	Data not accepted – see below
3		90	Data Accepted	Data not accepted
4		43.6	Error Message 'Please enter a whole number between 0 and 90'	Data was accepted
5		Smith	Error Message 'Please enter a whole number between 0 and 90'	As expected
6		99	Error Message 'Please enter a whole number between 0 and 90'	As expected
7		91	Error Message 'Please enter a whole number between 0 and 90'	As expected

It is not good enough to state whether or not the test was successful, you need to document the results of the test to provide evidence.

Usually the best way of doing this is to take a screen shot of the test being carried out and annotate it to show the results. You then need to describe any corrective action that was taken and repeat the test to show that the corrective action worked.

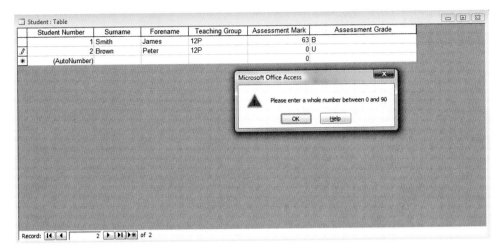

Fig. 7.3 *Test 1 and Test 2 outcomes*

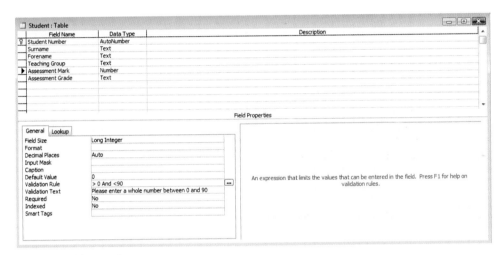

Fig. 7.4 *Validation rule wrong*

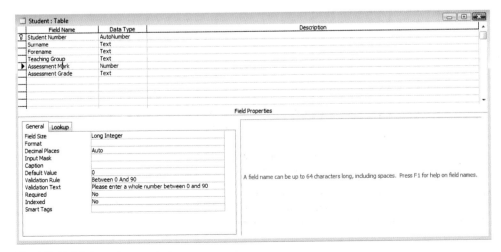

Fig. 7.5 *Validation rule corrected*

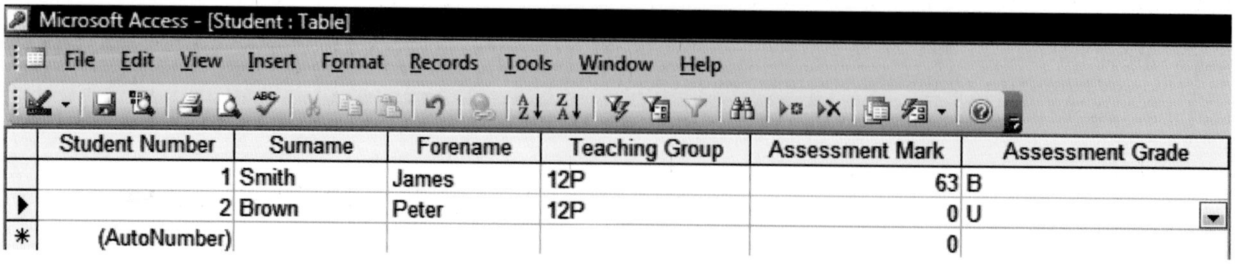

	Student Number	Surname	Forename	Teaching Group	Assessment Mark	Assessment Grade
	1	Smith	James	12P	63	B
▶	2	Brown	Peter	12P	0	U
＊	(AutoNumber)				0	

Fig. 7.6 *Test 2 now OK*

As you go through your test plan, you are building up evidence of how well your solution works, what it did well and what it failed to do. This is important evidence to quote when you evaluate your solution.

AQA Examiner's tip

You are expected to take evidence of testing you have carried out into the examination with you. Your sample work should include a test plan and clearly annotated samples of testing evidence that is cross-referenced to the test plan.

■ End of sub-topic questions

3 Describe what is meant by the terms normal, extreme and erroneous data and give an example of how they would be used when testing a solution.

4 You have completed a brochure for a local hotel which advertises their party services, and have printed out a final draft copy. The brochure includes a tear-off enquiry slip that potential customers can return to request further information. Make a list of tests you would carry out on the brochure before you handed it to your client for their approval.

☑ *In this section you have covered:*

- identifying the sub-tasks you need to carry out when implementing a solution
- planning your time so that you complete the work on schedule
- documenting your implementation
- designing a test strategy
- planning your testing
- choosing test data
- testing validation rules
- involving the client, end user and audience in testing
- documenting testing results and corrective action.

8 Evaluation

In this section you will cover:

- comparing a solution with its specification

- assessing the effectiveness of the solution

- suggesting improvements or enhancements.

8.1 Assessment of the effectiveness of solutions

It is important to evaluate the success of the solution that has been produced and assess how well it solves the problem it set out to address:

- Does the solution do what it was supposed to do?
- Does it do it in the way it was supposed to do it?
- Is the solution an effective one?
- If it isn't, then what is wrong with it and what would make the solution an effective one?

Your evaluation needs to be based on more than just your personal opinion. All the important aspects of performance should have been covered in your test plan, and evidence of the solution's successes and failures should be presented in the testing section. You should refer to these as you write your evaluation, and make sure that you include failures as well as successes. Making your evaluation a realistic one sometimes feels strange; it isn't easy to criticise something you have spent a lot of time on, but it is an important skill to learn as it helps you prepare for future work.

Does the solution do what it was supposed to do?

One of the important documents produced at the analysis stage of the work was a list of the client's requirements. The logical way to answer this question is to look at those requirements and assess how well each has been met in the finished solution. Was the requirement met completely, partially or not at all?

Some of the requirements will have been quantitative and should be fairly easy to assess; for example, if the requirement was that it should take less than 15 seconds to load a webpage, your testing should have proved whether this requirement was met or not. This is a good reason for making requirements quantitative whenever possible. Qualitative requirements, such as whether a blog was interesting and exciting for the audience may be more difficult to assess, and may have to rely on opinions gathered from a relatively small sample of people.

For example:

Specification statement	Evaluation
The solution must produce a total price for a computer based on the motherboard, amount of RAM and hard disk space the user chooses plus the cost of any extras the user wishes to add. The totals calculated must be 100% accurate.	The user could choose the motherboard, RAM and hard disk space, but I had to restrict the number of extras that were included to a limited range to avoid the input screen getting too complicated. The solution then produced a total price based on all the choices. The total was 100% accurate in every example tested.
The intranet pages should inform the students what food will be on the menu in the school restaurant each day and encourage them to eat healthily.	Looking at the access log records proved that a lot of students looked at the menu pages, and I worked hard to promote healthy eating by making the healthy food look really attractive. I can't really judge if they actually chose healthier food when they got to the restaurant though, but I can ask the manager about the sales before and after.

The sound effects must be appropriate to the spoof horror theme of the play and be easy for the sound operator to find and load.	After I had mixed the sound effects, I got the director to listen to them, and she suggested some changes which I built in. I made sure that the sound effects were all numbered to match the cues in the script so that the sound crew only had a single button to press for whatever sequence of sounds they wanted at that point. After they had tested the solution, they said that the sounds loaded quickly and were very effective.
The leaflet must be suitable for parents who wish to book a party. They must be able to fill in a slip that tells the party organiser exactly what food and facilities they want.	The leaflet did include a slip for parents to fill in, but they often found they didn't have enough space to fill in the information because I had made the boxes too small. The leaflet really needs to be redesigned to allow more writing space.
The solution must produce a bill for all the stationery bought by the pupil to be charged to their end-of-term accounts. The data entered must be 100% accurate and so must the total price.	By using a bar-code reader and their library card, entering student data was 100% accurate. Making a bar-code list of all the items for the staff to scan made that 100% accurate too (we checked the list very carefully), but it would still be possible to input the wrong quantity sold, so I suppose it was about 90% accurate overall.

Fig. 8.1 'I really liked my sound effects but my end user would have liked the option to turn them off'

Activity

Choose a website and write down what you think its designers set out to do. Design a questionnaire to assess what 10 other people think of the site. Based on that evidence, write an evaluation of how well you think they have achieved their aims and how you think they could improve.

Does it do it in the way it was supposed to do it?

Before the solution was implemented, design sheets were produced to communicate how the problem was going to be tackled. In practice, it is quite likely that these designs have changed as the solution has been implemented, perhaps because:

- The original design didn't work.
- A better method suggested itself as the work was being carried out.
- The client changed their mind about what they wanted, perhaps as a result of seeing the implementation as it was worked on.

There is nothing wrong with a design changing to improve the final solution. In practice, it would be rather surprising if the designs did not change, at least a little. Even experienced designers will change the way they do things if they have a better idea while working on a solution. The fact that you may be working with a piece of software with which you have limited experience makes it even more likely that your first design may change as you implement it. Similarly, your client may not have realised that certain things were possible, and showing them a solution in its early stages may make them think of another feature that would be useful. The important thing is that these changes in design should be documented, saying what changes were made and why they were felt to be necessary or desirable.

In your evaluation, you should explain what changes you made to your design and why you made them. For example:

'I originally used a nested IF function to calculate the discount the customers were entitled to, but I then realised that a lookup function would mean that they could change the values more easily, and so I changed to that instead.'

'When the client saw how useful the chart that analysed the sales by product was, he asked if I could also analyse them depending on who sold them, so I added this chart to the presentation for him.'

Is the solution an effective one? If it isn't, then what is wrong with it and what would make the solution an effective one?

The first question to ask in this section is what we mean by effective. We use all sorts of products on a regular basis, and most of them work. It is also true to say that some of them work better than others, and those are the products we would judge to be more effective. Exactly what makes a solution effective will naturally vary depending on the problem being solved, but the following list will apply to many solutions.

How long does it take?

It is never enough to state that a solution does something quickly, because speed is relative. Does the solution do its job more quickly than the method the client used to use? Does it meet a time target set in the original specification? If this is an important requirement, the testing plan should have included tests to measure, for example, how long a webpage takes to load or how long it takes to enter a customer's order into a database.

'My specification said that it should take no longer than 30 seconds to find a customer record in the database. It took much less than that on my database, but it wasn't really a fair test because I didn't have a realistic amount of data stored, and that could slow the access speed down quite a lot.'

Fig. 8.2 *'The large size of the graphics and video files meant that I did not meet my target that the page should download in 30 seconds'*

Key terms

Efficient solution or control: one where the user does not waste time or effort when using it.

Default value: one that a control is set to unless changes are made to it; for example, a paper size may be set to A4 unless the user chooses a different size.

How efficient are the controls?

If the user has to make lots of key strokes or mouse clicks to perform a task, it may be an indication that the solution is not particularly **efficient**. For example:

■ If the user of an interactive system has to move through lots of pages to get to the information they want, it may mean that the navigation was not designed well or that a search feature might have been necessary.

■ If a user has to enter the same data over and over again, it might have been better to set a **default value** to the field, or use a drop-down list or radio buttons to choose from the options available.

■ If a user repeats the same sequence of tasks, a macro might have allowed the sequence to be performed with a single mouse click or keyboard shortcut.

■ If the task requires the user to swap between mouse and keyboard regularly, it may slow the process down. Perhaps the controls could have been grouped more effectively or made better use of icons or keyboard shortcuts.

For example:

'My specification said that the person viewing the website should never be more than two clicks away from the information they were looking for, but the way I designed the site meant that sometimes the users got stuck on pages with no obvious way to get back. I really need to redesign the navigation bar so that the user gets to the information more quickly and can always get back to the home page with a single click.'

'Nearly all the products the company make are made from aluminium, with just a few in other metals. I used a drop-down list so that they could choose which metal, but it would have been better to have set the default value to "aluminium" so that most of the time they don't have to choose at all and they can just change it when they need to.'

How intuitive is the solution?

Your end-user testing should give you an impression of how easy the user found the system to use. An **intuitive solution** should mean that the user did not need to consult the user guide very often because the steps needed seemed logical and obvious. Improving this might be as simple as producing clearer labels on navigation buttons or building in help features such as tips that appear when a user hovers over a control.

For example:

'I asked my user to fill in a questionnaire about how easy he found the database management system to use, but I also watched him while he tested it. He only needed to refer to the user guide twice, both times to see how to print some of the reports. I found by renaming the reports to titles that he recognised, it was easy to overcome this and so I think that means my solution was quite intuitive for him to use.'

■ **Remember**

Pressing mouse buttons or keys over and over again can cause health and safety problems. Good interface design keeps the user healthy as well as speeding up the task.

■ **Key terms**

Intuitive solution: one that feels natural and logical to the user.

Fig. 8.3 *'I thought my solution was quite intuitive but my end user found it much more difficult to use than I expected'*

■ **Activity**

Choose a piece of software on your school or college computer system that you have not used before (your teacher may be able to suggest the best one to choose).

1. Try to use the software without using help features such as tutorials. Write a short report on how intuitive you found the software to use and which features were particularly easy or difficult to learn to use.

2. Look at the help files, tutorials and any other user support provided with the software. How good were they? Was it easy to find help for specific features? Add your verdict to your report.

How accurate is the input data?

In most solutions the user will be inputting data, and keeping data-entry errors to a minimum is vital to ensure that the information output is accurate. The evaluation should assess how well validation and input controls helped to reduce errors, avoiding the need for the user to re-enter data to correct mistakes.

For example:

'I used tick boxes and drop-down lists on the web form as much as I could to make it quicker to fill in than typing the answers. This also cut down on mistakes, because the customer couldn't choose a travel destination the company didn't offer. I also used a presence check on important fields. If the customer had left one of them blank when they pressed submit, they were just returned to the form to fill in the missing values.'

How efficient is the processing?

In most software packages there is usually more than one way to build a solution. You should try to assess how well you used the tools that were available or whether another tool might have done the job better. For instance, a well-designed macro might carry out several instructions at once rather than the user having to carry out each function individually.

For example:

'I used the automatic animation tool to make the character move across the screen, but it never really looked very realistic. I really needed to go back into the animation and create some extra frames in some parts to make the motion smoother.'

How appropriate are the outputs?

Whether the output is on screen, through speakers or on paper, you need to judge whether the solution produced outputs that were what the client wanted. Did documents look attractive and fit in with house style? Did the voice-over encourage customers to look at the presentation? Did longer documents break between pages in a way that still left them easy to follow?

For example;

'My report looked fine when I first tested it, but when I added more data so that it needed to print on several pages, some problems became obvious. The headings only appeared on the first page, so the other pages were hard to make sense of, and records for one person sometimes split across two pages so you couldn't look at all their information at once.'

How robust is the solution?

There are few things more frustrating than using a piece of software that freezes or fails to function when certain tasks are carried out, which means that the solution is not **robust**. It is important to note whether your user experiences such problems as screen freezes or error messages when macros are running. Sometimes these problems are not immediately obvious, and perhaps will only show when a large amount of data has been entered or the user does something unexpected that was not part of the original test plan.

■ Key terms

Robust solution: one that works reliably without failing or causing system errors.

Fig. 8.4 *'The design of the sales report was not as well laid out as it should have been and so it printed on too many sheets of paper'*

One way of supporting the user in case the system crashes and corrupts the data is to include a backup strategy in the user guide to help the user recover a previous version.

For example:

'The data transfer macro wasn't completely reliable. Every so often it stopped working properly, and then it gave a run-time error that was hard for the user to get out of. I never really did track down what stopped it working, and this is definitely something that needs to be investigated and improved.'

Summing up

Having looked at all the aspects of your solution in detail, it is useful to sum up the most important findings and prioritise any actions you would take to make the solution more effective. It is also worth reflecting on the overall process by asking yourself what changes you would make to your approach if you were asked to attempt a similar task in the future. Would you still use the same software? Would you change the techniques you used? Would you allow more time for particular sections of the work? Was the original brief a good choice or was it perhaps too simple or unrealistically difficult?

If you felt your basic solution worked well, could it be developed further, perhaps to do extra tasks that the client would find useful? If so, what developments would you recommend and how would you go about doing them?

Evaluating your own performance is a useful way of improving any future work you carry out. Did you plan your time well? Did you let deadlines slip because you didn't work hard enough, or did you only fall behind when things went wrong? Did you work well with your client and do you think they would be happy to work with you again? Did you feel your own skills were sufficient or do you need to develop them further before attempting A2 project work? Answering these questions honestly will help your personal development and make future projects easier to tackle.

AQA Examiner's tip

Look carefully at the number of marks awarded for each section of a question. Many 2-mark questions require a point to be stated plus some further explanation. Go through your answer and ask yourself where the examiner would tick the first point and where they would tick the expansion.

Activity

Discuss the following statements from student evaluations. How useful do you think each one is?

1 'My spreadsheet isn't working as well as I wanted it to because my computer at home broke and it took us three weeks to get it fixed.'

2 'The version of the leaflet I ended up with is actually the one I liked least. I think it's too bright and the fonts are too heavy, but my client really preferred that one.'

3 'My dad was really pleased with the website and he said it did everything he wanted it to do.'

4 'My specification said that the database would make a list of all the appointments for each stylist every day. I didn't do this because my client said she didn't really need it and it would make it too complicated to use.'

☑ *In this section you have covered:*

- evaluating the solution against the list of client- and end-user requirements to assess whether each one was met completely, partially or not at all

- evaluating the methods and techniques used to judge whether the right approach was chosen and the correct tools and techniques used

- evaluating how effectively the solution works, judging whether it:
  - is intuitive to use
  - has accurate input data, as far as possible
  - processed the data efficiently to produce the desired outputs
  - was robust enough to stand up to regular use

- evaluating your own performance, assessing your strengths and weaknesses so that you can use that knowledge to make a better job of the next project you undertake.

AQA Examination-style questions

Section 1: Input

1 A webcam is a video camera that captures images, which can be transmitted across the Internet. Describe one way in which a company can make use of this technology to benefit its business. *(2 marks)*
AQA, 2004

2 State three ways of entering text into a document when using a word processor. *(3 marks)*
AQA, 2003

3 A company has offices on five different sites; each office has between 10 and 20 members of staff working in it. Internal e-mail is used as a means of communicating between the staff. It has been suggested that speech recognition input and voice output might be used for the e-mail system.

   (a) State the extra input and output devices each PC would need to support speech recognition input. *(2 marks)*

   (b) State two advantages to the staff of using a speech recognition system. *(2 marks)*

   (c) State three reasons why the speech recognition system may not be effective. *(3 marks)*
AQA, 2002

Section 2: Output

1 A school has decided that the four printers on its local area network need replacing.

   (a) For one type of printer that the school might consider purchasing:
     (i) name the type of printer *(1 mark)*
     (ii) give one capability of the named type of printer *(1 mark)*
     (iii) give one limitation of the named type of printer. *(1 mark)*

   (b) For another type of printer that the school might consider purchasing:
     (i) name the type of printer *(1 mark)*
     (ii) give one capability of the named type of printer *(1 mark)*
     (iii) give one limitation of the named type of printer. *(1 mark)*

   (c) Should the school purchase four new printers of the same type, or should it purchase two different types of printer? What would you recommend and why? *(2 marks)*
AQA, 2006

2 Many business people need to have Internet access and office support applications such as word processors and spreadsheets when working away from the office. Name three portable devices that offer such facilities. For each device explain what a business person might use it for and why they might choose that device over the other two. *(9 marks)*

Section 3: Storage

1   Raj has a home computer that he uses for college work, photo editing and downloading music. For each of the following suggest what storage media he should use and justify your choice:

(a)   Send copies of his holiday photos to his aunt in India.   *(2 marks)*

(b)   Take his essay into college so that he can continue working on it.   *(2 marks)*

(c)   Take a backup of his entire system.   *(2 marks)*

2   DAT tape, removable hard drives and CD-Rs can all be used for backup purposes. State one situation for which each type of medium would be suitable and explain your choices.   *(9 marks)*

Section 4: Software

1   A local charity runs a toy library that allows parents to borrow educational toys for their children to play with. They need to be able to store details of the parents in the scheme and the toys they borrow.

(a)   Name the type of software that would be most suitable for solving this problem.   *(1 mark)*

(b)   State and explain four features of this type of software make it a good choice for this solution.   *(8 marks)*

2   Database management software can be used to solve many different problems.

Describe a problem that you have solved using database management software and explain how the functionality of the database management system software helped you to solve that problem.   *(6 marks)*

Section 5: Health and Safety

1   Poorly designed computer workstations can lead to health problems. State three features of a well-designed workstation, and for each one state the health risk that could be reduced.   *(9 marks)*

AQA, 2005

2   In order to protect the health and safety of the end user, certain factors should be considered when designing a piece of software. State four factors that should be considered, giving a reason for each one.   *(8 marks)*

AQA, 2002

3   'Health and safety at work is everyone's responsibility.' Discuss this statement with regard to the use of ICT systems and software.   *(8 marks)*

Section 6: Analysis and design

1   Every ICT task involves the input of data, which is processed and then information is output. Using an example of an ICT task with which you are familiar:

(a)   State what the task is.   *(1 mark)*

(b)   Give one example of data that is input, stating how it is input.   *(2 marks)*

(c)   Describe one process needed to fulfil the task.   *(2 marks)*

(d)   Give one example of information that is output, stating how it is output.   *(2 marks)*

AQA, 2006

2   Items stored in a computerised stock control system are uniquely identified by a product code. The format of the product code is XX9999, where:

X – Capital letter (A, B or C)

9 – Digit

The product code has a range from AA1000 to CC9999.

Name and describe three validation checks that could be used on this product code.   *(6 marks)*

AQA, 2006

3   Explain the difference between the terms verification and validation when applied to the input of data. Illustrate your answer with an example of each.   *(4 marks)*

AQA, 2006

4   A business manager is responsible for running a large office with 10 computer workstations used to input data sent in by customers. She has asked you to review the system they use and suggest possibilities for improving it.

List three techniques you might use to gain further information about her requirements and discuss the suitability of each of them.   *(9 marks)*

Section 7: Implementation and testing

1   (a)   Explain two possible sources of error that can occur when data is entered into a computer system.   *(4 marks)*

(b)   Name two methods of reducing data-entry errors, and state how each method is used.   *(4 marks)*

2   A company takes hotel bookings over the Internet. An online reservation form has to be completed.

(a)   State three fields other than Surname, Address and Postcode that you would expect to find on the reservation form.   *(3 marks)*

(b)   Name and describe a suitable validation check for each field that you have chosen.

All your validation checks must be different.

(6 marks)

AQA, 2005

3   Using the evidence you have brought with you into the examination, discuss your test strategy and the main types of test you have carried out.   *(6 marks)*

Section 8: Evaluation

1   Choose one of the requirements you have stated and discuss how you could evaluate it.   *(4 marks)*

2   Select a test from your test plan that shows your solution does what it is supposed to do. Explain how you could use the results as part of your evaluation.   *(4 marks)*

UNIT

2   Living in the digital world

Sections in this unit:

9 ICT systems and their components

10 Data and information

11 People and ICT systems

12 Transfer of data in ICT systems

13 Safety and security of ICT systems

14 Procedures for backup and recovery

15 Uses of ICT systems

16 Factors and consequences of ICT

Introduction

In our digital world, ICT delivers a number of different technologies to many areas of life and individuals and organisations inevitably feel the impact of instant communication, vast storage space and immense processing power. The aim of this unit is to allow you to look closely at the impact ICT is having on society and see it from a much deeper perspective. Each unit within the module will try to focus your mind on how ICT works and the effects that it is having.

This unit looks at ways in which ICT has been integrated into, and also changed, society and the way in which it works. A large number of jobs already require ICT skills and many more will follow as organisations integrate technology into their day-to-day tasks. The first two sections start at the basic level of how all computer systems involve input process and output, and then consider that data is processed to produce information that is output in various different forms.

Sections 11 moves on to consider that ICT systems are designed to be used by different people and many different factors, such as experience, physical characteristics, environment and the task that the system is being developed for. It provides an understanding of the skills needed to work in the ICT industry.

Section 12 gives you an understanding of transfer of data, different kinds of network, their uses and the standards that exist for their use, and Section 13 looks at safety and security, how data in ICT systems needs to be protected, through legislation, from both internal and external threats. You must be able to differentiate between malpractice and crime and understand that legal action will be taken in the event of security breaches. Section 14 discusses the need for regular backup to ensure recovery if disaster strikes, and the different media that are available to make the backup. Organisations have a duty to ensure that there is an allocation of responsibility for backup to ensure continuity of service.

The last two sections look at the uses of ICT systems and the factors and consequences of ICT. The various benefits include fast repetitive processing and vast storage capability and the facility to search and combine data. ICT does have limitations in what it can be used for however, and does not always provide the most appropriate solution. Finally you will look at the fact that there are different forms of processing including batch, interactive and transaction, and that all ICT systems are influenced by cultural, economic, environmental, ethical, legal and social factors. These combine and ultimately have a consequence for both individuals and society.

Specification	Topic content	Page
ICT systems and their components	What is ICT?	94
	What is a system?	94
	What is an ICT system?	95
	Components of ICT systems	97
Data and information	Data and information	102
	Coding and encoding	102
	Processing data	105
	Quality of information	105
People and ICT systems	ICT systems: design and purpose	108
	Characteristics of users	108
	How users interact with ICT systems	111
	Working in ICT	115
Transfer of data in ICT systems	What is an ICT network?	120
	Characteristics of a network	121
	Use of communication technologies	126
	Standards	127
Safety and security of data in ICT systems	The need to protect data in ICT systems	131
	Threats to ICT systems	133
	How are ICT systems protected?	134
	Legislation to protect ICT systems	136
Backup and recovery	Backup	142
	Recovery	148
Uses of ICT systems	What ICT can provide	153
	Is the use of ICT systems always appropriate?	157
	Types of processing	159
Factors and consequences of ICT	Factors influencing the use of ICT systems	162
	Consequences of the use of ICT	167

ICT systems and their components

In this section you will cover:

■ what is meant by the term ICT

■ systems and ICT systems

■ component parts of an ICT system.

Although ICT systems can be made up of various components, they all involve the three stages of input, process and output. In this section, you will learn to identify these stages in a system. You will also study the components of an ICT system in some detail so that you understand the part they play and how they all link together.

9.1 What is ICT?

Information and Communications Technology is the use of technology for the input, processing, storage and transfer of data and the output of information.

We tend to think of this in terms of traditional computers doing tasks such as sales processing by entering sales data to produce output information, such as an invoice. In practice there are far more options available, using laptops, PDAs and mobile phones. Digital TV sets can be used to take part in interactive quizzes, shop electronically and check e-mail, using a familiar interface that people feel comfortable with.

9.2 What is a system?

The word 'system' does not just apply to computers, it applies in many areas of science and engineering, but all systems have the three basic stages of input, processing and output. A system can be paper-based. In a restaurant, for example, there needs to be a system in place to record customer orders (input), put all of the prices for the separate items together and add up the total the customer has to pay (process), and finally produce the bill (output). Some restaurants already use computers for this process and in the modern digital world many are introducing computerised billing systems.

Input–process–output

The stages of **input, process and output (IPO)** form the basic functions of a computer system. A simple explanation of how this occurs:

■ Data is entered via an input device, such as a keyboard.

■ Calculations, queries and other operations are performed on the data in the processing stage.

■ The results of the processing are sent to an output device such as a monitor.

The following diagram shows one of the ways in which IPO works.

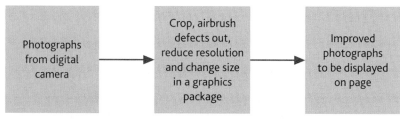

Fig. 9.1 *Input, process and output*

Did you know?

It is possible to buy fridges that have built-in monitors and connect to the Internet.

Key terms

Input, process and output (IPO): input is the capturing of data, process is converting the data into information and output is the information produced.

AQA Examiner's tip

Data is a plural word (the singular word is datum), and so when you give examples in an examination, make sure they are plural. Saying that the data input to a system is the examination mark will not gain marks; you need to say that the input is the marks for the students taking the examination.

Activity

Try drawing other IPO diagrams that might be used in ICT systems. Choose a piece of software with which you are familiar and draw an IPO diagram for a task you would use that software to perform.

End of sub-topic questions

1 Schools and colleges need to input and process attendance data on a daily basis.

  a Describe what output information is produced from this data.

  b Draw an IPO diagram to show the system.

2 Write down the input, process and output for each of the following:

  a finding contact details in a PDA

  b buying a book from a website.

3 A bank creates a monthly statement for each of its customers' accounts, which is an output from the system.

  a List the data that must be input to the system to produce the statements.

  b Describe the processing involved in producing the output.

Did you know?

Expert systems or knowledge-based systems are computer programs that analyse data about a specific type of problem. The knowledge base and the rules by which it is processed are designed by experts in the field and an interface is provided so that the user can extract the information they need. NHS Direct is a good example.

9.3 What is an ICT system?

ICT systems are those where the output from the system goes directly to a human being or into another ICT system.

How and why organisations use ICT systems

ICT systems meet particular organisational needs. You need to learn how to identify the components used in an ICT system and describe their contribution to the overall purposes of the system.

Most modern organisations use ICT systems to help them fulfil their goals, but the exact nature of the ICT system will depend on what those goals are. It is commonplace for many organisations to use ICT systems to produce information that would traditionally have been produced by paper-based systems. This might include receipts, invoices, sales, reports and wage slips. Other ICT systems have been created for situations which would have been impossible without the processing speed of modern computers.

Case study

Driver Vehicle and Licensing Authority

The DVLA website has replaced a system that was formerly paper-based in order to improve efficiency and convenience. In the past, most drivers purchased the tax disc for their car by visiting a post office, presenting their documents and paying a fee. Now drivers who visit the DVLA website can purchase their tax disc online without the need to travel to the nearest post office and wait in a queue.

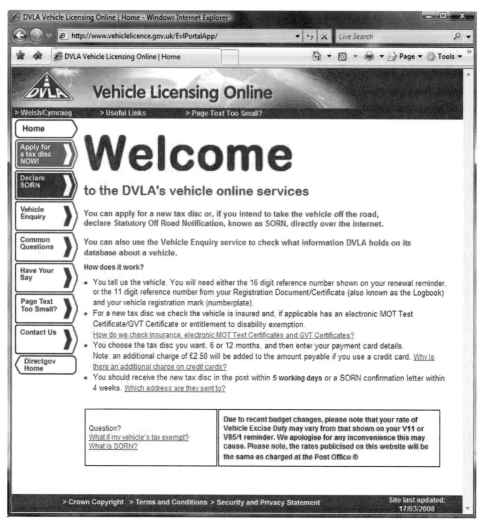

Fig. 9.2 *Applying for car tax online*

■ Did you know?

It is expected that 40 per cent of retail sales in the UK will be made via websites by 2020. Such sales made up only 2 per cent of all UK sales in 2002, but had reached 15 per cent in 2007, with total sales worth around £40 billion. This increase in online shopping and the need for efficient and accurate online ICT systems has never been greater. Consumers will only use these ICT systems if they actually save them time and money.

Check out the latest figures to see how consumers' habits are changing in response to new ICT technologies at:

Report: UK online shopping to grow by 40 percent by 2020 www. financemarkets.co.uk by Elaine Frei, 16 February 2007.

The customer needs either the 16-digit reference number shown on their renewal reminder, or the 11-digit reference number from the Registration Document/Certificate (also known as the 'logbook') and their vehicle registration mark (number plate).

How does the DVLA check insurance and the MOT Test Certificates?

When the customer applies for a tax disk on the DVLA website the vehicle's insurance will be electronically checked with the Motor Insurance Database (MID), run by the Motor Insurers Information Centre (MIIC). The database also checks that the vehicle is insured and, if applicable, has a new-style MOT Test Certificate. The change to a computerised system of MOT checks in garages has allowed for the move to online vehicle licensing.

You can find more information about the MOT computerisation project, and new-style MOT Test Certificates by visiting the Vehicle and Operator Services Agency website, at www.vosa.gov.uk

9.4 Components of ICT systems

The following are the components of an ICT system:

- people
- data
- procedures
- software
- hardware
- information.

People

No ICT system can work without people being involved at various stages. The first stage will be in the analysis, design, implementation and testing of the system, which will be carried out by systems analysts and programmers. As Section 6 explains, these systems are built to suit a particular client, end user or audience, and the computer specialists will work to meet the requirements of the client. Systems are much more likely to succeed if the clients and end users are involved at every stage.

Large organisations are often divided into departments that carry out the four main functions of business. They make use of ICT systems in all aspects of the business:

- sales – processing transactions involving the sale of goods or services provided by the organisation
- purchasing – processing transactions involving the purchase of goods or services required by the organisation
- finance – managing the flow of money in and out of the organisation, planning investments and managing accounts
- operations – carrying out the main business of the organisation.

Departments communicate and exchange information with each other, and with external bodies such as customers and suppliers. This will be done using various types of ICT process, including:

- e-mail and other ICT-based communication systems
- finance, payroll, budgeting/forecasting using spreadsheet or special-purpose software
- stock control using relational database management software
- marketing of products and services, often done online using websites.

Networks and intranets can help workers to communicate and share data to produce an efficient organisation even if some of the workers are on the opposite side of the world.

Data

The definition of 'data' is raw facts and figures or a set of values. The following are some examples of data that might be input:

- 25, 30, 45, 60
- Jones, Smith, Parker
- A, B, C, D, E

It is important to remember that the definition of data is plural. Data can be input by different input devices, as described in Section 1:

Did you know?

The UK is in the midst of an IT skills crisis and desperately needs quality workers. There is growing evidence of a worsening skills shortage. Since 2001 the number of students studying computing in higher education has dropped 40 per cent and is showing no sign of recovery (*Computing*, 15 February 2007). This decline is threatening UK research and the future of the IT industry and Gordon Brown has warned that the basic IT skills of UK staff fall short of European rivals (*Computing*, 8 February 2007).

■ keyboard

■ bar-code reader

■ scanner

■ digital camera

■ microphone.

■ Procedures

If an ICT system is to work effectively, it is important to have procedures in place. Most organisations have a code of practice which governs the way in which their ICT system can be used by their employees. All laws and legislation that have been introduced by government must also be taken into account when using the ICT systems. These include the Data Protection Act, Computer Misuse Act, the Copyright, Designs and Patents Act (covered in more detail in Section 13) and the Freedom of Information Act. Users must ensure that they follow security procedures such as the use of user names and passwords and anti-virus software should be used to check removable media brought in from home to maintain the integrity of the ICT system. These breaches of procedure for employees can be dealt with via the company's ICT code of practice as they form an integral part of it.

■ Software

Software packages are the programs that make the computer a useful tool by carrying out the processing. As Section 4 explains, the choice of software will depend on the system being implemented. The choice must ensure that the software can produce the desired output from the system. This choice could be made from a variety of packages including word processors, webpage design packages, spreadsheets, database management software, desktop publishing and presentation packages. Special-purpose software such as accounting packages may also have their place in the organisation. Sometimes an organisation may need bespoke software to complete a specialist task that generic software would not be suitable for.

▮ Hardware

■ Key terms

CPU: the Central Processing Unit, is sometimes just referred to as the processor. In computing power terms, the CPU is the important part of a computer system where most calculations are carried out.

ALU: Arithmetic and Logic Unit – where calculations are done.

IDU: Instruction Decoding Unit.

Control Unit: provides the means of communicating with the machine.

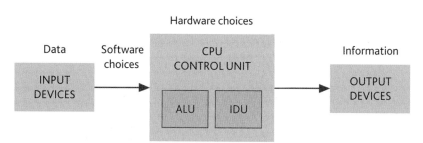

Fig. 9.3 *A computer system*

The type of computer and peripherals chosen will depend on the type of processing and output that is intended for the task. Storage space and processing power are two of the key aspects that will be taken into account when making choices about the hardware that is chosen. Specialist output devices such as colour laser printers may also need to be taken into account when looking at the task that the ICT system is performing.

Main components

You must be able to identify and know the purpose and characteristics of the main hardware components of an ICT system including:

- input devices, e.g. keyboard, mouse, scanner, bar-code readers
- processors, e.g. CPU
- output devices, e.g. printer, speaker, monitor
- ports and cables, e.g. parallel, serial, universal serial bus (USB)
- storage devices, e.g. hard drive, rewritable CD (CD-RW), DVD-RW, memory sticks.

For more on these components see Sections 1, 2 and 3.

Information

The final output is the information produced. Information is data that has been processed into something that is meaningful. An example of information might be a chart produced to show the average grades achieved by A Level, AS Level students taking an ICT course. This graphical representation shows in a clear and understandable way how the information can be used to review the performance of the class as a whole.

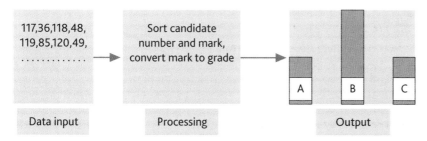

Fig. 9.4 *Chart produced to show class performance*

Data and information will be explored in greater depth in the next section.

Case study

IATA

The International Association of Travel Agents is introducing e-ticketing for all travel agents that are within their association. This is a good example of how an ICT system uses input, processing and output to produce a solution to a problem using the latest technology. The data concerning the passenger will be input, including personal details and flight details. These will be checked for the best available flights and, when chosen, the passenger will then pay using a credit/debit card. The details will be processed in the airline's ICT system to ensure that the correct flights are booked. No paper output will be given to the customer as they will verify who they are at the airport and be issued with a boarding pass. The organisation believes that the following benefits will arise through the use of this system:

- no more paper stock to manage or printers to maintain
- no more courier or mailing fees for sending tickets

■ no more airline fees for using paper tickets

■ better customer service.

All of the above will make a difference to the organisation by helping them to meet their aims or increase profits.

Fig. 9.5 *E-ticket on a mobile phone and electronic ticket reader*

Case study

E-ticketing trial at Arsenal and Manchester United

The new system of ticketing involves the use of a ticket being texted to the supporters' mobile phone. They input the type of ticket they want, it is then processed by the club and the output is texted to the supporter's mobile phone. This text ticket has a bar code which is scanned at the turnstiles, then goes through a validation process to produce the information required to allow the supporter to gain entry and take up their seat.

End of sub-topic questions

4 Many travel agents feel that the use of e-ticketing has benefits for them.

   a Discuss whether you think there are benefits to the customer generated by the use of e-ticketing.

   b Discuss any limitations you think there might be for the travel agents or the customer.

5 What ICT systems do you use on a regular basis? Discuss and make notes on the various different systems that you and your immediate group come into contact with.

6 Get together in small groups and think about the following:

   a What are the components that make up a particular ICT system?

   b What similarities can you see as being part of those systems?

   c Are there any obvious differences between systems?

   d Do you work at evenings or weekends in an organisation that has an ICT system in place? If so, what components make it up?

☑ *In this section you have covered:*

■ Information and Communication Technology is the use of technology for the input, storage, processing and transfer of data and the output of information

■ systems consist of input, output and processing

■ in ICT systems, the output goes directly to a human being or into another ICT system

■ ICT systems consist of several components – people, data, procedures, software, hardware and information.

10 Data and information

In this section you will cover:

■ what data and information are

■ different types of data

■ coding and encoding

■ processing data

■ quality of information

■ information as a commodity that has value.

We are in an information age where data is collected in many different ways on a regular basis about all of us as individuals. It is important that we understand what happens to this data when it is processed to produce information that many different individuals or organisations can use for various purposes.

ICT systems input data which is processed to convert it to information.

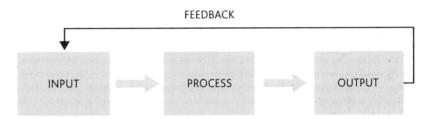

Fig. 10.1 *Input, process, output and feedback diagram*

In some systems, the resulting output is fed back into the system, modifying the input until the correct output is produced.

If good-quality information is produced, it can be used by humans to aid the decision-making process.

An Industrial Society to an Information Society

The birth of an information society, and the death of the old industrial society, is the most important 'megatrend' – one that is still not universally recognised as a reality.

In the past, those who controlled capital controlled the world, but in an information society the 'world controllers' will be those who control information.

Having access to the facts is not the key; everyone receives more or less the same information. In fact we are drowning in information, but often starved for knowledge. The trick is to filter out correct knowledge; to pull useful information from the endless sea of computerised data.

Megatrends, John Naisbitt, 1982

The extract above uses slightly different language to the way we might express it, but it is certainly true to say that many organisations have huge amounts of data available to them that could provide useful information if it were processed correctly. It is also true to say that many people are presented with huge amounts of information that is of no relevance to them. A good information system will present each person with information that is useful to them in a form that makes it easy for them to use.

10.1 Data and information

💡 What is data?

Data represents raw facts and figures or a set of values. You may be familiar with gathering data in some of your other subject areas, such as geography, where data might be collected using a questionnaire.

A set of data might consist of 2, 4, 3, 5, 6.

Another familiar set might be data collected from examination results, such as 23, 45, 67, 98, 78.

💡 Types of data

Data can arise in other formats as well as text and numbers. It can also take the form of still or moving images, or sound.

Bits and bytes

Whatever the type of data being input, computers store and process data using binary numbers. A single unit in binary is called a 'bit' which stands for binary digit.

Computer memory is measured in 'bytes'. One byte is made up of eight bits. One byte can store one character; for example, the letter A is represented by 01000001, B by 01000010.

See Section 3 for more information on bits and bytes and the relative sizes.

10.2 Coding and encoding

Encoding and coding data

When data is collected it may need to be **encoded**. An example would be for fields on a paper-based document.

It is often necessary to **code** data in order to be able to process it effectively. Value judgements are a good example of this. If as part of a survey you ask 100 people how good they think a restaurant is, they could all give a different answer, and that would be very hard to enter as data in order to analyse it further. If they were asked to rate the restaurant on a scale of 1 to 5, where 1 is excellent and 5 is very poor, a single digit needs to be fed into the computer and the fact that it is a number makes it an easy way to compare that restaurant with another one included in the survey.

Encoding data

Encoding is used by computers to convert the data into machine-readable form. All computers understand is binary, 1s and 0s, but this is difficult for humans to understand. Therefore, in order for people to use computers, the data that they use must be encoded into binary for a computer to process and share, i.e. encoding our language into machine-readable form.

A way of encoding text is by using ASCII to represent each character as a binary number.

The following are examples of the binary codes that make up the letters and numbers that are assigned to the QWERTY keyboard.

AQA Examiner's tip

Remember that data is plural (the singular is datum), so if you are asked for an example in an examination, you could quote 23, 45, 67, 98, 78, but not just 23.

These data strings do not have any meaning on their own, but they can be input to a computer system to be processed into information.

Key terms

Encoding: used by computers to convert the data into machine readable form.

Coding: some data is coded on collection before being entered and this changes the original data into a shortened version by assigning a code.

Symbol	Decimal	Binary
A	65	01000001
B	66	01000010
C	67	01000011
D	68	01000100
E	69	01000101
F	70	01000110
G	71	01000111
H	72	01001000

Coding

Some data is coded before storage and this changes the original data into a shortened version by assigning a code. When data is coded it is essentially done to keep it short, which saves storage space, but it speeds up data entry.

Some codings that you may be familiar with are:

Gender: M or F for Male or Female

Questionnaire answers: Y or N for Yes and No

The colours of the circles could be said to be blue, red, green, brown when coded and not the original colours of vivid red, royal blue, emerald green or pale brown.

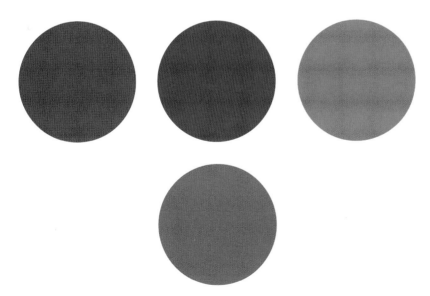

Fig. 10.2 *The circles when coded are simple colours*

In the above example there is only one choice for any shade of blue, and any other shade would still be coded as blue. This means that when the data is coded it loses some of its accuracy but it does take up less memory on the system. However, codes can be difficult to remember; imagine remembering your favourite book by its ISBN (International Standard Book Number) rather than its title!

Bar codes

A familiar set of data that you, or certainly the main shopper in your family, will have come across are the bar codes used in supermarkets. They also play a leading role in stock control and customer ordering for web-based commerce in warehousing. They are seen in the form of a UPC (Universal Product Code) and come in several varieties, but the most common in the UK are EAN 13 (European Article Number 13 digit) and EAN 18. A series of bars and spaces represent the code numbers which are read by a bar-code scanner.

Bar codes are very versatile and have the advantage of being able to be read from different angles and even when upside down. One of the key features is that an automatic check is made for any data-entry errors using validation. All products have a unique number which is allocated by the European Article Number Association. There are no details of the product stored in the number only a country of origin and a sequence code. The bar code has stood the test of time and looks likely to remain the standard form for coding and automatic data capture for many applications although RFID is increasing in popularity. Some examples of the application of bar codes include student cards and products in warehouses and, of course, supermarkets. This might be when the product details are identified from searching the company's database after scanning at a point of sale. The output will include the product description and price which will be shown on the monitor and printed out in a receipt. In a supermarket the database is usually developed and maintained by the individual retailer so it can be customised and changed to give more details on the product, including price. An interesting example of bar code use is when blood samples are taken from athletes to determine whether illegal drugs have been used. Each sample would have a bar code attached to ensure its authenticity.

Fig. 10.3 *A bar code*

Another coding system that is seen on most printed books is known as the ISBN. This is similar to a bar code and all books have a unique number which is a composite code. Most books have their ISBN number printed on them in bar code format, making stock control easier than traditional methods. If you look on the back cover of this book you will see an example of one.

Most text-based data is entered into computers manually through keyboards, but there are many different data-entry methods, which you will find described in more detail in Section 1.

ISBN 10: 1-932698-18-3
ISBN 13: 978-1-932698-18-3

Fig. 10.4 *Example of an ISBN*

End of sub-topic questions

1 List three forms that data being input to a computer system can take. For each form of data, give one input device that can be used (re-read Section 1 if you get stuck).

2 Give two reasons why bar code regconition has have become such a popular data input method for the retail industry.

3 State three examples of data.

4 Describe the problems that may be encountered if data is coded.

10.3 Processing data

What is processing?

Processing is the work the computer does on the data to convert it into information. This might involve calculations, logical operations such as sorts and queries or changing the shape of a sound wave to make a sound lower or higher in pitch.

What is information?

A computer is a data-processing machine. Computers process data to produce information. Information is data that has been processed into something that is meaningful. For instance, in a supermarket the data from the bar code is processed to produce a receipt with the item names and prices included.

Fig. 10.5 *A supermarket loyalty card*

For example, examination results might be represented by a graph that clearly shows the different percentages that students in a particular class have achieved. The raw examination marks could have been entered in as data, the processing would involve converting those marks to standardised scores and allocating the appropriate grade before presenting them in graphical format. This information makes it easier to assess the performance of the group than using the raw data.

Supermarket loyalty cards capture data when they are used. The customer number, date and time of purchase and codes of products bought are captured when the card is used at the checkout. The data can be processed to provide information about purchasing habits, and the supermarket can use that information when deciding what special offers might tempt you to spend more at the store.

10.4 Quality of information

What makes information valuable?

Information is a commodity, which means that it can be bought and sold, and therefore it potentially has value.

Information has increased value when some or all of the following are applied:

Accuracy

The information on a sales report must be accurate to the exact monetary value otherwise any decisions made will be inaccurate. This is extremely important as organisations need accurate information to remain in business.

Thorough error checking must take place and regular updates must be applied if the information is to remain accurate.

Up to date

Some information only has value within a specific timescale, for instance share prices can change several times in a minute, and so buying recommendations that are produced would change quickly and have no value at all once they were out of date.

Information produced on consumers' tastes will invariably change and organisations must ensure that they have up-to-date information. This would be particularly important for organisations ordering stock to sell to customers. If the stock is reordered based on out-of-date information it is highly likely that profit margins will be affected if stock is left unsold.

Complete

If the information is not complete then it loses its value.

If the information produced about a householder for insurance purposes does not include the amount of money the house is being insured for then it is incomplete and loses value as the house will not be insured for the correct amount.

From a reliable source

Because of the lack of control on the content included on Internet websites this can often reduce the value of the information obtained.

Individuals are often encouraged to obtain their information from trusted sources like the BBC websites or trusted newspapers or other recognised organisations as opposed to online resources which are written ad hoc by users, such as Wikipedia. It would certainly make sense to look at reviews if you were buying a new computer. Computer magazines regularly test and report on equipment from a variety of manufacturers, and these provide valuable information which is more likely to be impartial than information from the manufacturers.

Relevant

Information is only valuable to someone who has a use for it, and its value will also depend on that potential use. For example, if a company has information on a summary sales report then it must show sales of individual members of staff if it is to be relevant for calculating staff commission bonuses.

Did you know?

Census data prior to 1901 is available free of charge on microfilm at most local archive libraries. Family-tree researchers usually prefer to pay for the same information in online electronic format, because it is easier to search and available at any time they choose to access it.

Fig. 10.6 *Satellite navigation systems provide drivers with accurate, relevant and up-to-date information based on data from satellites*

End of sub-topic questions

5 What is the difference between data and information? Illustrate your answer with an example.

6 Some companies/institutions hold data about you, from which they can draw information.

   a Which organisations store data about you?

   b Why do they keep that data?

   c Do they sell it?

   d What control do you have over it?

7 When you finish a set of external examinations, you are issued with the information of what grade you achieved in each.

   a What data was fed into the computer system to produce that information?

   b What processing was carried out to turn the data into your final grade?

☑ *In this section you have covered:*

- data – what it is and what forms it can take
- information – what it is and what forms it can take
- the factors that affect the value of information
- the difference between coding and encoding
- the fact that data is plural and is input into ICT systems
- examples of information in relation to the use of ICT systems
- the concept of input, process and output and being able to give examples that relate to ICT
- the different types of data that can be input into an ICT system.

People and ICT systems

In this section you will cover:

- systems are designed for different types of people or end users

- what the characteristics are of users of an ICT system

- how users interact with an ICT system

- the types of jobs that are available in ICT

- the skills required to be successful in the ICT industry.

Activity

Do some research into ICT systems and find some examples of both those that have been successful and those that have not.

11.1 ICT systems: design and purpose

As with all practical applications of ICT the systems that are used by organisations have been designed to be used by people and commissioned for a particular purpose.

When you consider the design of an ICT system for a particular purpose, it is important to appreciate that different users have different needs (Section 6 on analysis and design covered how to identify these needs). The client, end user and audience may all have slightly different requirements from the system, and each of their requirements need to be considered. The analysis of user needs is critical in determining the requirements of the system, because if the system designed does not take these needs into account sufficiently, it is unlikely to be successful. It is also important to ensure that the solutions provided to clients are aligned with changing business needs. It is, therefore, essential that the link with the client and end user remains live throughout the project.

There are many examples of systems that have been implemented that have failed to meet the requirements of the people who commissioned them. There are many different reasons for this. One of the most publicised examples was the London Ambulance System, which failed to do the job it was meant to do. Key factors that have to be taken into account when considering a new system include:

- Ensuring the cost of implementation is worth the benefits it will bring (sometimes known as 'cost benefit analysis').
- Timescales for implementation. These must be realistic and allow time for thorough testing.
- The need to involve clients and end users to ensure the system meets their needs.
- The requirements of the client and end user. These have to be realistic and clearly stated.

11.2 Characteristics of users

Users of computer systems will vary considerably in the way they interact with computers. This interaction may be affected by such factors as:

- experience
- physical characteristics
- environment of use
- task to be undertaken
- age.

Users vary considerably in their requirements from any system. Some may be computer experts, others novices. They may have strong preferences for the type of interface they like or the hardware they prefer to use. They will have different degrees of skill and experience and different psychological attitudes to change. Some users may have particular needs due to physical impairments. It is up to the systems analyst to establish the needs of the user and to pass those on to the system designer so they can be taken into account.

Fig. 11.1 *People use computers in all walks of life*

Older users may react more slowly than younger ones, and so the ability to adjust the speed of cursor movement and the rate at which they need to double-click an icon can make a large difference to their confidence, especially when they are novices. Having said that, the fastest growing group of Internet users is said to be the older generation of 'silver surfers' who have time available to follow hobbies and interests using their computers.

Environmental factors can also affect interaction considerably. A designer working in a quiet office is more likely to want the sound effects of the software he is designing played through headphones rather than speakers. A computer sited in a noisy factory probably needs visible rather than audible output, as audible output may not be heard over background noise, and headphones may not be feasible if workers need to talk to each other.

The task to be undertaken will naturally affect the **user interface**. An operative in a busy restaurant might find a concept keyboard interface very useful for entering items in an efficient manner by touching a picture icon for each item on the menu. A graphic artist will probably

Key terms

User interface: the link between the user and the technology that they are using; involves both hardware and software.

prefer to use a graphics tablet rather than a mouse to provide a more natural drawing experience.

Figs 11.2 to 11.5 show some different types of user interface.

If a variety of users need to use the same interface, it may be desirable to allow them some degree of customisation over some aspects of it so that experienced users do not feel that the system slows them down, and novices do not feel that they cannot cope. Keyboard shortcuts may be very useful to expert users, for instance, instead of having to click their way through layer after layer of menus to find a feature they use regularly.

An example of an ever-expanding area for interface design is in e-commerce where the design might include a web interface for customers placing orders. The designer will have no way of knowing the likely level of expertise of each customer, so it is quite a demanding

Fig. 11.2 *TVedia's media centre user interface*

Fig. 11.3 *iPhone user interface*

Fig. 11.4 *A future interface projected into thin air?*

Fig. 11.5 *Mori user interface*

task to put together a robust interface that is simple and efficient. A system should give the customer clear guidance regarding what they need to do, and any data entry needs to be validated, offering choices, i.e. drop-down lists, rather than free text wherever possible to avoid data-entry errors. Menu-driven interfaces are often effective for systems that are used by the general public. Many facilities are available to make websites more accessible, such as text descriptions for important pictures that can be output as sound files to help visually impaired users.

No system can be foolproof and it is also important for online help to be provided. This help function must also be well designed – users must be able to navigate through clear search options that describe system functions and potential problems clearly, without using unnecessary technical jargon. In every aspect, the system must be easy for customers to use or they will simply give up and shop somewhere else.

11.3 How users interact with ICT systems

Users interact with ICT systems through the hardware and software components of the user interface. Most standard systems rely largely on a keyboard, mouse and monitor for their interface, although as previous sections have shown, many other input and output devices can be used to suit particular circumstances.

The most common interface type is the **graphical user interface** (GUI). The standard convention of left-click to select, right-click for information and double-click to load means that users can usually use the basic functions of software without too much difficulty, especially if the icons are clear and well designed. Generally speaking, developers use similar icons to represent familiar tasks, although a standard set of icons is not used by all software manufacturers, there are similarities. Fig. 11.8 (overleaf) shows an example set of icons used in a Bibliographic Database user interface.

Key terms

Graphical user interface: most commonly used type of interface; uses icons or pictures that are easily understood by the user and can be clicked using an input device. They vary between manufacturers but are generally seen as the most intuitive way of using a computer, giving access to users with different levels of knowledge.

Fig. 11.6 *Mac OS X*

Fig. 11.7 *Microsoft Vista*

Icon	Meaning	Icon	Meaning
🏠	**Home** Return directly to the Welcome page/screen	📖	**Thesaurus** Browse the thesaurus for search terms which match the given search string
	Menu Display the main menu		**Limit** Reduce number of returned results by applying additional search criteria (e.g. Date of publication)
💬	**Change Language** Toggle between the native language of the site (represented by whatever is their flag), and English	⊣⊢	**Location** Display information about the selected object's location (e.g. a URL for a web page, or a shelf number for a library book)
ⓘ	**Information** Display information about this facility (e.g. database, search systems)	👁	**Show/View/Display** Show the results of the current search (Some systems will not automatically show results of a search but merely tell you the number of matched results
❓	**Help** Display help on the current task	🖨	**Print** Print the current item (e.g.) screen, document or search set)
🔍	**Find** Look or search for a particular set of documents	💾	**Save** Save or download search results to a file
📇	**Browse** Display an Index of access points (e.g. authors)		

Fig. 11.8 *Icons from Bibliographic Database Systems 1992 Project IT3/92*

Activity

Look at the examples of icons in Fig. 11.8. These were used for a IFLA IT Section GUI Standards Project Report Bibliographic Database system in 1992 Project IT 3/92. Some of the icons are still in use but, dependent on the software that you are familiar with, they may differ.

Which icons are still in use?

Which icons need changing to reflect the ever-changing ICT systems that are in use?

◪ Graphical user interfaces are for WIMPs!

Most GUIs make use of four basic features:

- windows
- icons
- menus
- pointers.

Menu-driven interfaces

Menu-driven interfaces can be useful in situations where the user needs to be restricted to a limited choice of actions.

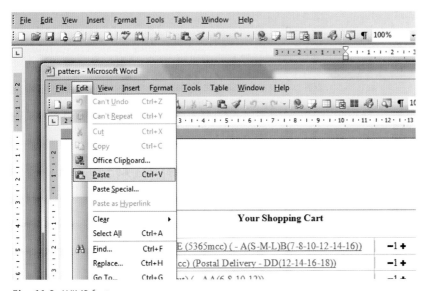

Fig. 11.9 *WIMP features*

Originally, menus were usually chosen by entering a single number or letter chosen from a simple text-based list. For example, press 1 for sales, 2 for stock control. This method is still used on many automated telephone systems, where the user moves through the menus by entering numbers on a touch-tone phone.

Many mobile phones use menu-driven interfaces where users choose options from the keypad, although some of them have now moved to GUIs using a tiny joystick to choose between graphical icons.

Another major use for menu-driven interfaces is for public information systems in shopping centres and railway stations. These often use touch screens as combined input and output devices because they need no keyboard or pointing device to be attached. There is more information about these in Sections 1 and 2.

Command line interfaces

Command-line interfaces (CLI) are not used very much by non-expert users, because they are more difficult to learn to use than the other types

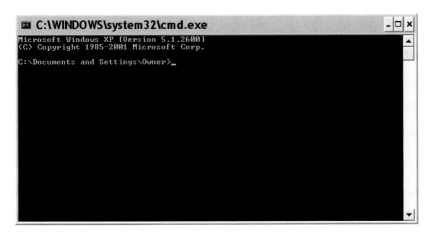

Fig. 11.10 *Command-line interface*

of interface. A CLI relies on the user typing in text-based commands for the computer to execute, and so the user has to know the commands in the first place. CLIs do not make heavy demands on system memory or hard disk space, and they can be quicker than graphical interfaces for expert users.

Interface design for effective communication

The most important factor to bear in mind is the principle of trying to make the interface fit the user rather than the other way round. That means that the designer needs to take into account the factors stated at the beginning of this section, including the task and the environment as well as the user themselves.

Section 5 of this book also explains how important the interface is to the health of the person using it. Interfaces that minimise the number of times a key is pressed or a mouse is clicked also minimise the strain on the users' wrists and fingers.

One of the goals that many researchers in the computer industry are working towards is that of a natural language interface. The idea of this is that users should be able to communicate with the computer in the way that they would speak normally, rather than having to choose special words and commands that the computer will understand. This would have to allow for poor spelling and grammar, slang and dialect words and the various ways humans say things. For example, in most households at least, if someone is asked to 'put the kettle on', they are expected to boil some water rather than wear a metal water container on their head! Building logical rules that can cope with the variations in human expression is an extremely complex task and there is still a long way to go before such interfaces become a reality in most situations. Having said that, the Ask search engine and the help systems in Microsoft Office both attempt to allow the user to type in a question rather than just the key words that are stored in the database.

Human beings have five senses – sight, hearing, touch, taste and smell – and in some circumstances an interface can be made much more effective by making use of them.

Taste and smell are not very practical, at least at the moment, however:

- Touch – simulators used for training can have sensitive gloves that respond to touch, as if the operator is taking part in a real event such as a medical procedure.

- Sight and hearing – multimedia tools such as sound and video can be used to demonstrate features of software, for instance, by showing and telling the user what to do next rather than the user having to work from text and diagrams.

Some packages allow the user to configure the user interface for themselves, adding and deleting the buttons from toolbars so that the features they use are readily available. Keyboard shortcuts may be available as alternatives to menu commands, speeding the process up for more experienced users. Smart menus rearrange themselves as you use them, so that frequently used options will move to the top of the menu.

⬕ Providing appropriate help and support for users

All users, whether novices or experts, will need help and support from time to time. As mentioned above, multimedia presentations can provide

Remember

Pre-school children use computers to learn from, and text is clearly not an option as most of these children cannot read. Spoken instructions and simplified input devices such as joysticks and concept keyboards mean that even very young children can interact with the computer and use it as a tool for learning.

tutorials to teach new skills, and many excellent software training packages build in the user's response to judge whether the user is ready to move on. There are many tutorials provided by software houses, by third parties and by user groups that use multimedia facilities to support new users learning to use a new piece of software.

The more traditional help supplied within programs can usually be accessed in two ways. There may be a search facility where the user types in the feature they need help with, or context-sensitive help may be available, where the help information offered depends on what the user was doing when they pressed the help button. For example, if the user was trying to set an input mask in a database management system, pressing help would bring up an article on input masks. This is often more useful, as sometimes the user does not know the correct term for the functions they need.

Another way of offering help is using a hover function. When the user moves the mouse over an unfamiliar control, the name of that control appears, perhaps with a further button to click for more help.

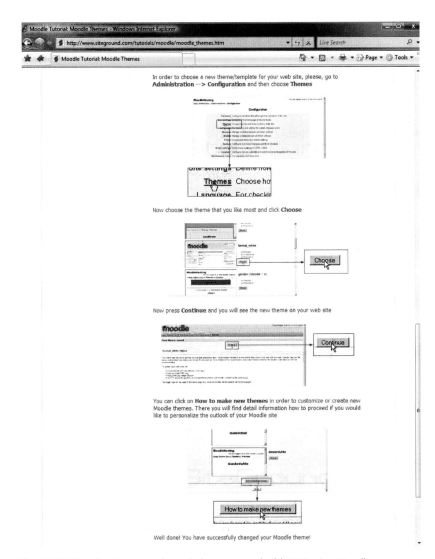

Fig. 11.11 *Step by step tutorials can help a new user build a VLE using Moodle*

■ Some benefits and limitations of user interfaces

Graphical user interfaces

GUIs tend to be user-friendly, making software more intuitive for inexperienced users. They can be frustrating for more experienced users, who may resent having to work through three or four levels of menu before they can use a feature they require. They are also quite demanding in terms of system resources such as hard disk space and memory.

Command-line interfaces

CLIs are generally reserved for expert users, as they demand considerable knowledge. The fact that they do not use graphics makes them far less demanding in terms of system resources than other interfaces.

Menu-driven interfaces

These restrict the options the user can select. This can be an advantage, for example, in interfaces for use by the public, but can slow down the use of the system as every user has to follow set routes. This means that they have to click on the appropriate choice at each menu stage and it can often take some time to reach the correct option. They are often combined with graphics and can be used effectively with touch-screen systems.

🔆 11.4 Working in ICT

There is growing concern that the UK is falling behind in the skills race, which could mean we do not have people with the right skills for the UK to compete effectively in the 21st-century knowledge economy, the sector of the economy that depends on the use of ICT systems for organising and managing information.

Contrary to some reports ICT skills are in demand and jobs are available.

> More than 150,000 of our technology staff are over 50 and are approaching retirement age. We are building a talent pipeline to ensure that we have staff with the right IT skills in place for the future.

Cheryl Baron, Recruitment and Diversity Programme Manager, Lockheed Martin, 17 Jul 2007

🔢 Jobs available in the ICT industry

Here are some job advertisements showing the skills required by real end users:

Activity

Read the two job advertisements opposite.

What personal qualities are demanded by both organisations?

```
• • • • • • • • • • • • • • • • • • • •
•                                      •
•        SUPPORT STAFF                 •
•                                      •
•    We are a market leader in regional newspapers  •
•     and direct marketing and now seek a well      •
•    qualified individual to join the support team   •
•       within our expanding IT Department.          •
•                                                    •
•   Supporting over 250 people, some remotely,      •
•     you will offer telephone and face-to-face     •
•    support, advice and problem solving – a total   •
•             help desk solution.                    •
•                                                    •
•    In addition to being a team player, you must    •
•    possess good verbal communication skills and    •
•   the patience to support users with a wide range  •
•                  of abilities.                     •
•                                      •
• • • • • • • • • • • • • • • • • • • •
```

Fig. 11.12 *Job advert for support staff*

Head of Digital Preservation

You will need to have the ability to lead a well-established team within the broader organisation of the archives. Clearly, you will need a good awareness of the technical issues surrounding digital preservation, but your personal qualities are far more important to us.

You will be supported by a highly skilled, multi-disciplinary team of twelve. You will need to liaise closely with colleagues and you will also be required to represent the organisation at a high level in external meetings.

You will have excellent written communication skills, as well as knowledge of the latest issues concerning information, records and knowledge management of digital records. You should be a strong team player with the confidence and ability to make difficult decisions when solving problems.

Fig. 11.13 *Job advert for a highly skilled managerial job*

Essential skills for the ICT professional

The technical skills required for any given job will change over time but the personal qualities remain the same. They include:

Good written communication skills

ICT professionals must have good written communication skills as they must have the ability to write technical documentation and end user guides. The ICT professional must take into account that the documentation will be read by end users with different levels of ICT skills from novice to very experienced. Clear language is essential if the users are to understand the documentation.

Good oral communication skills

ICT professionals must be able to communicate well orally so that they can communicate effectively with users or colleagues. An example of this might be the support job shown above, where it is important to find out exactly what the IT problem is and develop potential solutions. This skill involves the ability to ask appropriate questions and respond to the needs of the end user, taking account of the skill level of the user to ensure the professional has a full understanding of the problem. This skill is also important where an ICT professional would have to ask appropriate questions to get the correct user requirements to ensure that the correct system is implemented.

Problem-solving skills

The ability to analyse and solve problems is useful in many ICT jobs and working on a help desk and solving users' problems is an obvious example. If the ICT professional was trying to solve a user's software problems they would need to consider alternative solutions.

Logical thinking is essential for programmers and system designers – computers rely on logic to process data – and so the ICT professional must possess this skill in order to interact effectively with the computer, whether debugging a program or troubleshooting a printer problem.

AQA Examiner's tip

When answering questions about the personal qualities of people working in the ICT industry, you should not include technical skills, subject knowledge or experience, because these are professional rather than personal qualities and should be obvious from looking at a CV.

Patience

All ICT professionals need to have patience and be approachable to prevent end users from becoming flustered or anxious about the fact that they may have a lower skills base. They need to be able to stick at a problem in order to solve it and be willing to explain the same procedure several times until it is fully understood by the end user.

Activity

Research some of the ICT job websites such as www.eFinancialCareers.co.uk and www.cwjobs.co.uk

Complete the table below which includes an example of the personal characteristics required for the role of an IT database officer, as described. Use the table as a template and try to include a range of skills. By reading the job specification carefully, try to work out why that skill will be appropriate in that particular job.

'The IT Database Officer needs to have excellent communication skills, both oral and written. The IT Database Officer will be the first point of contact for all database related queries.'

ICT job	Personal characteristic 1	Reason for skill being important	Personal characteristic 2	Reason for skill being important
IT Database Officer	Good written communication skills	To write appropriate end-user guides that are understandable and are jargon free	Good oral communication skills	To interact with the end users and explain any problems clearly and in an understandable manner

Willingness to work flexible hours

This does not mean being willing to work different patterns or shifts of work, although some jobs may involve that, but is essentially being willing to see a task through until it is completed. ICT problems can take many hours to solve and the professional cannot just walk away and leave the problem at the end of their shift – organisations in the digital world rely on their ICT systems 24 hours a day 7 days a week and may lose vast amounts of income if they are not working properly. This may mean working extra hours when a particular task requires urgent attention.

Teamwork

Few ICT projects are completed by a single individual and so teamwork skills are vital, although the ability to concentrate when working alone may also be important in technical jobs such as programming. The results of that work, however, affect the rest of the team, and so everyone must work cooperatively, share information and support each other.

💡 Characteristics of an effective ICT team

The following list is not an exhaustive one, but it will give some indication of the factors that make a strong team:

■ The team leader must ensure that the team members work together in an organised and effective manner to ensure deadlines are met.

AQA Examiner's tip

It is essential to use the words 'good' or 'excellent' when answering exam questions regarding skills required. This is because it is assumed that many individuals possess similar skills but in order to be able to carry out ICT roles successfully they must have above-average skills. Answer using the phrase 'good written communication' rather than just 'written communication skills'.

Encouragement from the leader ultimately leads to a more motivated group.

- The strengths and possible weaknesses of all staff involved in the project need to be taken into account to ensure that the best possible knowledge and understanding are used to complete the ICT task; that is, tasks are allocated to staff who have the correct skills to complete them efficiently and effectively.

- An appropriate structure must be in place to ensure that the standard practices of the organisation are followed. This is important as team members may change due to unforeseen circumstances and any replacement to the team must be able to step in and carry on the project in as seamless a manner as possible. The way of working must be both structured and methodical and appropriate documentation (specification, design, test plans, user guides) must be produced and kept up-to-date ensuring that the documentation can be checked on a regular basis and that no requirements of the project are missed by mistake.

- There must be some form of monitoring of task progress to ensure that the project is completed to schedule as delays in projects can be very expensive. Monitoring will ensure that team members are working at the appropriate pace and remain aware of deadlines.

- It is essential that costs for completion of the project are monitored throughout to ensure that money has not been misused and to keep within budget.

- There must be a structure in place to ensure that the project continues to deliver what it set out to do in the first place. Some changes may need to be introduced, but the team should remain focused on its goals and the client's requirements.

- The balance of the team should allow people with different skills and knowledge to work together effectively, e.g. programmers, analysts, and designers, to maximise the efficiency of the team as a whole.

- All individuals within the team must possess good communication skills so that they are able to share ideas with each other and with end users outside the team.

Activity

Imagine you are the team leader for a project that is trying to create an invoice or report system (information system) for a large organisation.

Produce a presentation for your team members about the characteristics for an effective team.

In this section you have covered:

- the need to understand fully the design and purpose of ICT systems

- the different characteristics of users of ICT systems and how these affect system design

- types of user interfaces, their advantages and how this affects the way users interact with ICT systems

- some of the available jobs in ICT

- good written communication skills, good oral communication skills, good listening skills, problem-solving skills, patience and willingness to work flexible hours are essential characteristics for most ICT professionals

- teamwork and how team members work together successfully.

12 Transfer of data in ICT systems

In this section you will cover:

- what the basic elements of a network are
- characteristics of a network
- how networks communicate data and the use of communication technologies
- the standards used when communicating data.

Key terms

Computer networking: linking two or more computing devices together for the purpose of sharing data, communicating, software and peripherals.

Local area network (LAN): usually covers a single site and could be linked by the use of cables.

Wide area network (WAN): covers a large geographical area and could be linked by cables, microwave or satellites.

Metropolitan area network (MAN): covers an area like a town or city and could be connected by cables, microwave or satellites.

12.1 What is an ICT network?

You will have come across **computer networks** through your use of ICT in your daily lives and will be familiar with the role they play in your interaction with the hardware and software that you use. Networks are made up of thousands of different computing devices, made by different manufacturers and connected by different types of transmission media such as telephone lines, satellites and optical fibres. Traditionally some networks were local (**LAN**); a school site and some networks covered a wide area (**WAN**), which could reach across a country or even worldwide. The Internet can be described as the largest network in the world. Now the distinction between LANs and WANs can be blurred, and a new term, MAN, has been added. The factors to be considered are the difference in reach of the network and the difference in type of connection.

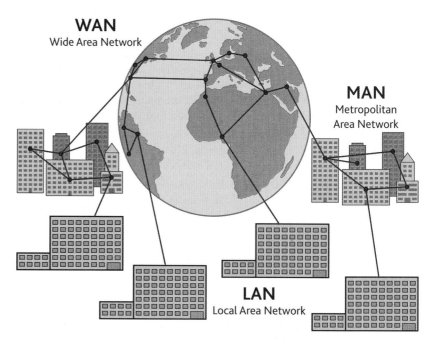

Fig. 12.1 *Distinction between a LAN, WAN and MAN*

💡 Advantages

Why use a network rather than just a standalone computer?

Activity

Write down all of the key advantages you can think of for using a network that you already know from your previous studies or experience.

There are many advantages for organisations and individuals of using networks that you are familiar with but may have taken for granted because you use them on a daily basis and have not thought about the consequences of what would happen if they were not available. The use of modern ICT networks has become so familiar and our dependence on them has reached a very high level. The main aim of networking computers together is to increase the efficiency and effectiveness of the work that they do within the system.

Sharing of resources

Have you ever really thought about what is going on in the ICT system when you sit at your computer and start to word process a document or create a database? When using a network you share the software resources from one drive and can then save your work to that network drive rather than locally on the computer that you are using. Peripheral hardware like printers and scanners can also be shared, saving time, by not having to go to a certain computer, and money, by cutting down on the number of peripherals that have to be purchased.

Communication

Intranets and extranets

An increasing number of organisations are now using an internal network known as an 'intranet' to communicate via internal e-mail and other methods like newsgroups. The individuals have access to the intranet where documents and templates that are used frequently can be accessed. The company may also have a bulletin board where messages can be shared between individual employees. This can be accessed at any time and reduces the need for the message to be sent to everybody in the organisation. The use of these resources will be governed by a code of practice that sets out how they should be used. Limited areas of the intranet can also be linked to the Internet and the use of e-mail facilities to enable effective communication with customers and suppliers and other people outside the organisation. Many organisations allow their staff to access the intranet from anywhere in the world, and many colleges and universities allow their students access to their intranet resources from home. Many schools and colleges also have a virtual learning environment (VLE), where students can access worksheets and upload assignments to course tutors via the Internet.

An 'extranet' is the part of an organisation's network that can be made available to outside users, for example customers or suppliers, giving them limited access to company resources and information. The security implications of this kind of access have to be considered carefully as it usually means that access is being made through the firewall, whereas an intranet stays securely within it. (Security will be looked at in more detail in the next section.)

■ 12.2 Characteristics of a network

ⓘ Network design

Peer-to-peer networks

At its simplest, a computer network is just two computers linked together so that they can share files and perhaps a printer. Each computer needs a network interface card and the connection is made either using a crossover cable or wirelessly. The operating system can be used to define which resources are shared and a basic network is in place. If more than two computers are involved, a **hub** could be used to provide the connectivity. This type of network is known as a 'peer-to-peer network',

Key terms

Hub: small, simple network device that allows multiple computers to communicate. Hubs are an inexpensive piece of network equipment often found in home wired networks and small businesses.

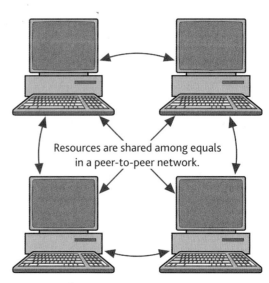

Fig. 12.2 *Peer-to-peer network*

because all computers on it have similar rights. This type of network does not need a dedicated network operating system; most modern operating systems have simple networking facilities that control the user access rights and file permissions.

As broadband connections have become more readily available, an increasing number of homes share their Internet connection between several computers by setting up a wireless LAN so that computers throughout the house can access the Internet at the same time. This also means that each computer does not need its own printer, and files can be backed up from one computer to another in case of equipment failure. The main computer connects to the Internet through an ADSL modem, and it is then connected to a wireless **router** that connects the other

Key terms

Router: hardware device (wired or wireless) that joins networks together at the network protocol layer.

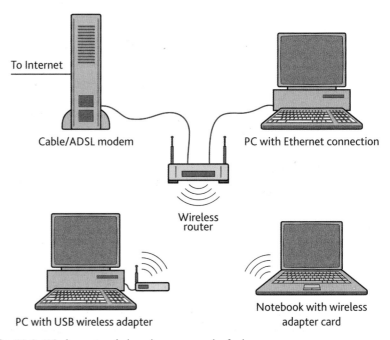

Fig. 12.3 *Wireless networks have become popular for home use*

computers on the network via their wireless network cards. Add to that the fact that many people routinely transfer data between their mobile phone and their computer using Bluetooth technology, and some home networks are really surprisingly sophisticated.

The same technology can be used in small businesses where central control of the network is not important. A peer-to-peer network can use all the computers connected to it as workstations, and so it is cheaper to set up than a client/server network which needs a dedicated server.

The use of wireless networks does bring security risks, however, and there are many documented cases of networks that have been set up without passwords and so have been accessible to the entire neighbourhood without the user realising it. Given the fact that many people buy goods and manage their finances online, insufficient wireless security makes identity theft much easier to achieve.

Client-server networks

In larger organisations, the network is much more likely to be server based than peer to peer. The server is a powerful machine, usually built to a high specification, using good-quality components because it forms the basis of the entire network. The server needs a specialised network operating system that enables it to manage complex sets of user rights and file permissions, for example, by splitting its very large file capacity into smaller virtual drives so that users can save and load files to their own directory without risking the security of other parts of the network.

Servers are usually fitted with RAID drive systems to ensure the data remains available to the network if a drive fails and its data becomes corrupt (see Section 3).

The server is connected to one or more **network switches**. Switches look nearly the same as hubs, but are generally more intelligent. They can inspect data packets as they are received and forward them efficiently to the connected device they were intended for. This conserves bandwidth and improves network performance compared to using a hub.

Each client, or workstation, that is connected to the network will need the client version of the network operating system to be installed. In many networks, the applications software is also installed on each workstation, as this reduces network traffic and load on the server. As you might imagine, if a large class of students all go into a room and load the same piece of software from the server at the same time, the network and server will slow down because of the increased load. If the software is installed on the workstation, only the data files are called from the server and the network traffic is greatly reduced.

In thin-client networks, however, all the software is loaded on to the server and most of the processing is carried out by the server too. This means that the server needs to be extremely powerful and the communication network needs a lot of bandwidth. The workstations, however, need only a very low specification so have a longer life because they don't need upgrading. Almost all modifications to the network, such as a software upgrade, will be carried out on the server rather than each and every workstation.

Client-server networks have some advantages over peer-to-peer networks in that they can be managed and backed up centrally and it is easier to concentrate resources such as security and maintenance on one main computer. Workstations are relatively cheap and easy to replace compared to a server.

Did you know?

In one 30-minute journey (using a Pringles can as an antenna to make signals easier to spot), witnessed by BBC News Online, a security company managed to find almost 60 corporate wireless networks, of which 67% had their encryption system turned off. (*Source:* http://news.bbc.co.uk)

Key terms

Network switch: hardware device that joins multiple computers together at the data link network protocol layer.

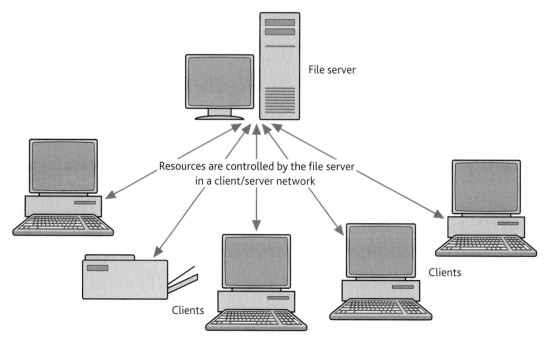

Fig. 12.4 *A client-server network*

End of sub-topic questions

This task can be done either in groups or individually.

1 What is meant by the term computer network?

2 Write down some of the advantages and disadvantages that a peer-to-peer and a client-server network might have.

3 Make a list of places where you have used a network and specify what type of network it was.

Case study – adapted from an article in *PC Plus* May 2006

Interconnected digital home

You may have read about Internet connected fridges and other weird and wonderful gadgets that would be part of the digital future but they hide the real ideas behind a home network that is either linked through traditional cabling or via Wi-Fi.

The possibilities for connectivity are real and involve the correct use of the technologies that are available to allow consumers to be able to listen to or view entertainment and run business applications around the home. It will be based around broadband connectivity and networked systems to allow householders to use their ICT systems in and around the home when and where they choose to.

The ICT system technology, of course, has to be available, which could include a digital TV, a media centre PC, a music system, a Wi-Fi network and other peripherals, dependent on each individual's preference. The next step is linking them all together. Will this define the digital home within the digital world?

Analogue equipment is quickly being replaced by ICT systems that have digital equipment that plays music downloads or play video or TV on demand. It also includes other technologies like e-mail, instant messaging, VOIP telephones, TV over broadband and also HD-DVD, Blu-ray discs, multi room audio systems and digital video recorders.

The system would include a central digital media server with a laptop, a set-top box and possibly a digital video recorder. There would be multiple digital media adaptor devices located around the house and linked together by a network server. The central unit might be capable of delivering recorded TV to a bedroom LCD screen, while piping audio to a music system, and making video and photographs available to other devices, in the same way that we call up data files from a computer server. This can only occur, however, when there is compatibility between all of the hardware that is purchased from different manufacturers.

The network that connects the digital home is key and the use of CAT5 or Ethernet cabling would be one way of doing it. A wired LAN would be very fast and would be able to pipe everything from audio to high-resolution video, supporting data speeds of up to 100Mbps, and rising to 1,000 Mbps for gigabit Ethernet. It also allows for a secure transfer mechanism. WI-FI is less intrusive in terms of décor but would have disadvantages for the speed of data transfer, particularly for video.

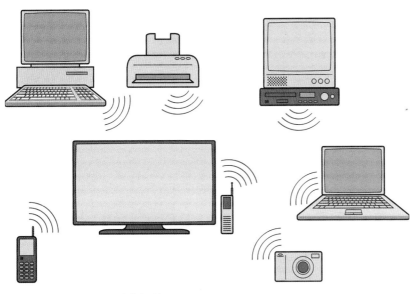

Fig. 12.5 *Interconnected digital home*

AQA Examiner's tip

If you are asked for a disadvantage of networking computers, do not state that data loading is slower than a standalone computer. This will not be the case if the network is well designed and powerful enough in terms of memory, processor speed and bandwidth.

Did you know?

By the end of 2005, 99.6% of UK homes were connected to a broadband enabled exchange capable of 1–2Mbps connection. Estimates suggest that by 2010, over half of all UK households will benefit from average broadband speeds of 10Mbps.

Research the new figures in the year that you are reading this.

Activity

Do some research in your class, school or college and find out what equipment individuals have in their home, how they use ICT systems at the present time and how they connect to the various networks that they use.

You may find out that many individuals are already downloading music, shopping online, using instant messaging and watching digital television. How important do they feel it would be to link these technologies together?

■ 12.3 Use of communication technologies

The Internet

■ **Key terms**

Internet: a large group of interconnected computers around the world that allow the sending and retrieval of information from one computer to another; sometimes described as 'a network of networks'.

You will already be familiar with using the **Internet** and it is important to understand the infrastructure that supports it.

Originally developed by the Advanced Research Projects Agency (ARPA), a US government agency, to allow university users to access research information from other universities, the Internet was set up so that even if some parts of the network were not working properly it would still be possible to use other parts and functions of the network. The Internet that you are familiar with links up untold numbers of computers and people using telecommunications networks that are already in place throughout the world. The TCP/IP set of standards (discussed later) is used to control their data transmission. The availability of the Internet has meant that

■ **Activity**

A small business with four standalone computers is thinking of setting up a network and has asked you to do some work summarising the benefits and limitations.

Copy and complete the following table giving as much information as necessary. Some have been filled in to help you get started.

Benefit or limitation	Explanation
Speed of communication	Networks can provide a very fast method of sharing and transferring files. If no network was available, files would have to be shared by using a storage device like a USB pen drive then carrying them from one computer to another
Cost benefits	
Centralised software management	
Sharing of resources, e.g. printers	
Electronic mail and Internet communications	
Access from anywhere on the campus or possibly home	
Expensive to install	Although a network will generally save money over time, the initial costs of installation can be prohibitive. Cables, network cards and software are expensive and may require specialist installation
Problems with cables breaking	With some networks a cable break can stop the whole network
Security threats are increased	
File server failure	
Increased administration time	
Any others of your own?	

users anywhere in the world can communicate with each other in a matter of seconds by using electronic mail. Many businesses and private individuals now use e-mail for much of their communication needs on a daily basis as it is convenient and inexpensive. Other communication methods include Internet relay chat and instant messaging.

The World Wide Web

The World Wide Web, www or the web, as it is often known, is the area of the Internet that you probably use now on a daily basis. It has become the main area for the retrieval of information stored on websites. Web browser software is used to access files through the use of HyperText Transfer Protocol (HTTP) which most web browsers and hardware platforms support. Webpages are usually written in HyperText Markup Language (HTML) and linked together using hyperlinks, allowing users to navigate between pages in a site and between one site and another. Until the World Wide Web was established, Internet resources were beyond the scope of any but the most technically minded of users. This increase in accessibility has led to the huge number of pages that we now see available. This in turn has led to an increase in the use of these resources for communication, shopping, banking and many other areas that would traditionally have been done in the locality in which you live or through more traditional communication links like the telephone.

> **Key terms**
>
> **World Wide Web (WWW):** a collection of multimedia resources accessible via the Internet.

12.4 Standards

De facto standard

A de facto standard is one where no formal agreement is in place, but a particular standard has become the one that is most commonly used in practice. Hardware, software, languages, protocols and formats that are widely used, but not endorsed by a standards organisation, can be judged to be de facto standards. The GIF format used for pictures placed on webpages is an example of a de facto standard that is widely used by web developers. The Windows operating system used in PCs is also widely perceived as an example of a de facto standard.

De jure standard

De jure standards are legally binding industry standards that all manufacturers have to agree to work to. Though they place restrictions on manufacturers, and some people feel this slows down development, these standards are beneficial both for the manufacturers and the end user, as adhering to them minimises compatibility issues. An example of a de jure standard is the wireless standard Wi-Fi, developed by the IEEE (Institute of Electrical and Electronics Engineers). Often standards start off as de facto standards and through acceptance and the fact that they work they become de jure standards.

> **Did you know?**
>
> The PDF format produced by Adobe has become a de facto standard for document exchange on the web. It has now been proposed that the ISO (International Standards Organisation) should adopt it as a de jure standard.

> **End of sub-topic questions**
>
> **4** Do you think that it is important to have standards or should manufacturers be allowed a free hand when designing and implementing hardware and software?
>
> **5** Do some research to find out more examples either de facto or de jure standards.

🖥 **PC activity**

Make a short presentation to either discuss why standards are important or why you think that creativity is stifled through the use of standards.

Protocols

The **Transmission Control Protocol (TCP)** and the **Internet Protocol (IP)** together manage the flow of data over the Internet.

A **protocol** includes formatting rules that specify how data is packaged into messages. It also may include conventions like message acknowledgement or data compression to support reliable, high-performance network communication. Many other protocols exist in computer networking, for example:

- HyperText Transfer Protocol (HTTP) – defines the process of requesting and transferring HTML webpages across the Internet. It also has a secure version, HTTPS.
- File Transfer Protocol (FTP) – allows users to send files between computers. A copy of the file is transferred to the receiving computer, and can be saved and its data read.
- Post Office Protocol 3 (POP3) – a popular protocol that defines the transfer of e-mail between computer systems.
- Secure Sockets Layer (SSL) – a cryptographic system for sending data, such as credit card details, securely over the Internet.

✓ *In this section you have covered:*

- the basic concept of networks and their advantages and disadvantages
- what intranets and extranets are
- peer-to-peer and client-server networks, and the advantages and disadvantages of each
- the Internet and the world wide web
- the standards that are applied to network technology
- protocols as a set of rules that govern communication over a network.

Key terms

Transmission Control Protocol (TCP): a protocol to manage the assembly (and reassembly) of data into packets transmitted between computers over the Internet; ensures reliable transmission; used along with the Internet Protocol (IP).

Internet Protocol (IP): a protocol which directs data from one computer to another.

Protocols: a set of known rules that govern the communications between computers on a network.

13 Safety and security of ICT systems

In this section you will cover:

- protecting data

- threats to data

- how systems are protected

- security of networks

- Computer Misuse, Data Protection and Copyright Designs and Patents Acts.

13.1 The need to protect data in ICT systems

As most areas in life increase their use of technology, it is more important than ever to use these advances to protect privacy and data. We need to ensure that data is available to the users who depend on it, but also that it is not misused by people who should not have access to it. Any organisation storing personal data is bound by the terms of the Data Protection Act, which requires data to be surrounded by proper security. Business organisations also wish to keep commercially sensitive data away from the eyes of competitors.

Fig. 13.1 *ICT systems need protection*

Did you know?

In 1890 Boston lawyers Samuel Warren and Louis Brandeis said in the *Harvard Law Review* that privacy was under attack by 'recent inventions and business methods'. They believed that privacy did not have to die for technology to flourish. This statement is still relevant today as technology is changing even more quickly, and privacy continues to be an issue foremost in many people's minds.

In the 21st century, where so many organisations are connected together, there are many external threats such as viruses attached to emails, electronic eavesdropping and electronic fraud. The security of networks within ICT systems is therefore extremely important. The explosive growth of ICT systems and interconnectivity via networks has increased the dependency of organisations and individuals on the data stored and communicated through these channels. In turn, the need to protect data and resources from disclosure to unauthorised bodies is now fully understood and the authenticity of data and messages must now be guaranteed to protect systems from network-based attacks. Cryptography and network security are constantly changing to create new weapons to enforce network security.

The introduction of the computer for data processing has increased the need for automated tools for protecting data stored on computers.

Network security measures are required to protect data during transmission. Virtually all business, government and academic organisations link up their data-processing equipment with a collection of interconnected networks. This, as we have seen, forms the basis for the Internet.

Government enterprises and private companies have recognised the need to protect their data, which is an essential part of the organisation. Any organisation with any major intellectual property to protect, such as film and book producers, software vendors and music producers, understand the need to protect their ICT systems. Smaller organisations may not realise just how important their data is until it's too late.

Activity

Intellectual property

Use an example of an organisation where its intellectual property is its main asset. This could involve software production, films or books, music or any other organisation you know about that needs to protect its data.

Think about what data needs to be secure and why it is important that the data does not become available to unauthorised people or organisations.

Make a short presentation to others in your group or write a short discussion paper to emphasise why the protection of the data is important.

Fig. 13.2 *A threat to security – a laptop left in plain view*

13.2 Threats to ICT systems

Employees

Although most people who consider system security automatically think of external threats from hackers and crackers, according to a survey conducted by the business advisory firm Deloitte it is estimated that over 50 per cent of threats to ICT systems are caused by the organisation's own employees. This could be caused by an employee selling confidential data for personal gain. Also, data could be lost and passed on through carelessness, for example if an employee leaves a laptop prone to theft in an unlocked car. An employee with sufficient security rights on a network can make copies of sensitive data quite easily and by using e-mail attachments or removable media, can pass them on to an unauthorised third party. An employee who is unhappy with some aspect of the organisation may also be a threat to its data by committing sabotage, such as deleting or corrupting important files.

Human error

The failure to follow standard clerical procedures can also put the security of data at risk. It is generally considered good practice for organisations to insist that users change their passwords regularly, and that security is increased if passwords have a mix of characters and numbers and don't use dictionary words. However, all of this breaks down if the passwords are so long and difficult that users can't remember them and they write them down and stick them on their monitors!

It is easy to forget that printed copies of information also need to be stored securely and shredded when no longer needed. Backup media have the potential to be stolen or copied, and will contain huge amounts of data. Again, they need to be kept in a storage area protected from unauthorised access as well as from physical dangers such as fire and flood.

Employees, then, can threaten data through **malpractice** or through **crime**.

Data privacy can also be threatened by the theft of the media on which it is stored and files can become corrupt if storage media become damaged. Computer hardware itself is relatively easy to replace, the same is not true of data stored upon it. Threats such as fire, flood and even terrorist attack can destroy buildings and equipment all at once, and if copies of the data are not available from a separate location the data loss may make it impossible for the organisation to recover from the event.

Viruses

One of the most publicised forms of attack on an ICT system is a **virus**. Sending a virus is not a bit of fun, but is actually an illegal activity. Some viruses do little or no harm; perhaps simply displaying a message on screen. Others can delete data or use up system resources to make the computer so slow it is virtually unusable. Viruses can be introduced by removable electronic media such as memory sticks or from an external source via the Internet, either via a download or from an attachment on an e-mail. Most systems have anti-virus software in place, but none are perfect, especially given the fact that new viruses are being written all the time. Once the virus is resident it can replicate itself to other files, and internal computer security tools are required to detect and recover from the virus. Most anti-virus software has an automated update system to check for new viruses.

Key terms

Malpractice: when an employee goes against the company ICT code of practice e.g. leaving a workstation logged on creating the opportunity for an unauthorised individual to access their account.

Crime: when individuals or organisations break the law through using computers to illegally access a computer system; e.g. to break in and change the payroll figures on the internal database.

Virus: a piece of malicious code that is written by programmers and used to corrupt data and systems. It comes in different forms, such as trojans, logic bombs and worms.

Fig. 13.3 *Viruses can do massive damage to computers*

■ Spyware

Increasing threats from spyware can lead to organisations' networks becoming more exposed to further attacks. Spyware is installed on the user's computer and is not always easy to detect. Some of the threats that it might cause are:

- Data that is stored on internal computer systems is sent to an external source without you even knowing and certainly without your permission.
- Passwords for Internet banking might be stolen, perhaps by the monitoring of keystrokes made by the user when logging on to the bank's website.
- Networks of infected computers could be used to commit further crimes over networks. This would allow hackers to control access to an organisation's computer system and give them access to all of the business transactions that are taking place.

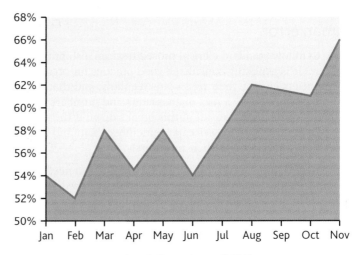

Fig. 13.4 *Spyware as a proportion of all new threats (2005)*

> ### ■ Remember
>
> A process of protection against a virus might consist of the following:
>
> - DETER – educate users about the dangers of viruses.
> - PREVENT – install anti-virus software, restrict removable media/downloads.
> - DETECT – update anti-virus software regularly and scan system frequently.
> - RECOVER – fix security weaknesses, restore data.

> ### ■ Activity
>
> Why do you think that individuals or groups might want to cheat and break into an ICT system?
>
> Complete the following table with possible reasons why ICT security might be compromised.
>
> | Security breach | Possible reason |
> | --- | --- |
> | Unauthorised access to data | To violate secrecy or privacy, such as … |
> | Impersonating another user | To withdraw money from someone else's Internet banking account. |
> | Changing functionality of software | |
> | Link into someone else's communication link | |
> | Claim to have either sent data or indeed not sent | |

End of sub-topic questions

1 It can be said that the biggest threat to an organisation's data is its employees. Describe two ways that the security of data can be put at risk by the staff who work with it.

2 Virus attacks can also threaten data. Carry out research to find out about any specific virus attack that has caused widespread corruption of data and write a brief report on the virus and its effects.

3 In your own words describe two internal and two external threats to the ICT systems.

Reasons for security breaches

Some of the reasons that individuals give for breaching security are:

- For the satisfaction of doing it – to try to show off to others and prove that they are skilled enough to breach security, almost as an intellectual game.
- Personal gain – for example, for a student to change their grades in an examination to achieve university entry.
- Financial gain – this might be the case if an individual were to change the bank accounts of a large number of customers by small amounts and add them all to their own account.
- Sabotage – to damage the reputation of a competitor's organisation by proving their security is weak.

Types of threat

- Data access threats mean that data is accessed while being communicated across a network illegally and is changed by individuals or organisations who should not have access.
- Service threats are designed to stop the data being used by the organisation it belongs to by disrupting the normal running of the software being used.

Viruses and worms are two examples of software attacks that can be introduced via corrupted media or via the Internet or attachments downloaded from an e-mail. The service threats can be contained in otherwise useful software.

Means of control of threat

Password-based login procedures are designed to deny access to all but authorised users and screening logic is designed to detect and reject worms, viruses and other similar attacks. Firewalls are designed to restrict access to intruders by securing data access ports. Secure Socket Layer (SSL) is used to encrypt sensitive data and increases customer trust when using websites – especially important for online retailers. Digital signatures are used to verify that a document is genuine and has been sent from a particular individual or organisation – included as part of an e-mail for example.

Data encryption

One way of protecting data is to encrypt the message by scrambling the data so that it cannot be understood if it is intercepted. An encryption key is used in conjunction with the transformation to scramble the message before transmitting and unscramble it when it arrives at the destination.

Key terms

Algorithm: list of instructions for solving a problem; in ICT and computer science, usually means a small procedure that solves a recurrent problem.

Conventional encryption

■ Plain text or original message is fed into an **algorithm's** input.

■ A secret key is input to the algorithm and all transformations and substitutions depend on that key.

■ The encryption algorithm performs various substitutions and transformations on plain text.

■ A ciphertext scrambled message is produced as output.

■ To decipher the message, a decryption algorithm is run. It takes the ciphertext and the same secret key and produces the original plain text message.

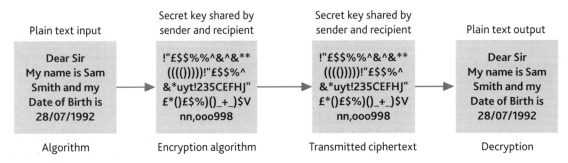

Fig. 13.5 *Simple model of conventional encryption*

Other examples of encryption can be found at websites including www.cs.usask.ca where you can try out some different types of encryption online.

End of sub-topic questions

4 Describe some of the reasons why individuals or organisations might try to breach the security of ICT systems.

5 Name two types of threat to ICT systems.

6 Describe a means of protecting data that is being transferred over a network.

■ 13.3 How are ICT systems protected?

The measures that can be taken to try to protect all parts of ICT systems, including networks, against threats are:

■ hardware measures

■ software measures

■ procedures

■ or a combination of any of the above.

■ Ways of protecting ICT systems

Hardware measures

Removable media can be a major threat to the security of data, and it is important to decide what devices are fitted to the computers. It is possible to specify computers that have no CD or DVD drives to ensure that no important data is removed. USB ports may be needed for other devices such as printers, but it still may be possible to use security software to set up a list of allowed devices and so prevent unauthorised use of these ports. This means that it is not easy to make unauthorised copies of data, and any files introduced to the network must be virus checked and approved by the network manager.

The theft of a computer also means that the data stored upon it is no longer secure. Computers can be fixed to work surfaces or locked in cabinets, and restricting access to computer rooms using ID methods such as smart cards or simple locks and alarms out of hours will also increase the security of the hardware. Biometric technology such as fingerprint or retinal scans can be used instead of keys or smart cards, or instead of passwords for network log on.

Software measures

Network operating systems have security functions built in, such as the allocation of user names and passwords, to control access and try to prevent **security attacks**. These also control the access rights the user has once they have logged on – which files they can see and what they are allowed to do to them. They may be allowed read-only access, or to add new data but not delete existing data. These access rights can be applied to directories or to individual files. For instance on a college network, a student may be allocated full control over their own directory, read-only access to departmental directories and no access to staff directories. A staff member might have full rights over their own directory and that of their department and no access to student directories. Files within the staff directory may be set with different levels, so that the user could edit certain documents whilst others remain read-only. The system can also control or block downloading and uploading files to and from the Internet.

Network security software can be useful to track down security abuses of the network. It can be set to record which user logged on to a specific computer at what time and date, when they logged out, what files they accessed and even what they did to those files. It can also generate warnings if a user repeatedly enters an incorrect password, as this may indicate that an unauthorised user is attempting to access the system.

Software can also be set to automatically save files every few minutes or each time a new record is entered or to insist that the user saves before closing. This can prevent loss of data caused by the user forgetting to save.

As described above, data encryption can protect data as it is transmitted from one computer to another, and anti-virus software is an essential part of any network security system. Firewalls should be in place to reduce the possibilities of the system being attacked by hackers.

Procedures

It should be made clear to employees during induction training what their responsibilities are as regards data security, and the penalties for breaking the rules. It is particularly important to define backup procedures and allocate responsibility for taking and storing backup files.

If security procedures are in place and staff are trained to follow them, security risks are much reduced. These procedures should form part of the company's ICT code of practice and an employee's contract of

Key terms

Security attack: any action that compromises the security of data held by the organisation.

Remember

Files can be set with access levels, for example:

- no access
- read-only
- read/write
- read/write/delete
- full control.

AQA Examiner's tip

Do not use one-word answers, e.g. 'passwords', for questions about security precautions. You must explain what you mean; for example, 'Each authorised user should be given a password to use to access the system and forced to change it regularly.'

employment will state the legal requirement of their job. Induction training should cover security procedures, and breaches of procedure should be covered by disciplinary procedures.

13.4 Legislation to protect ICT systems

The speed at which ICT systems have become the main component of many organisations has meant that laws to protect individuals and organisations have now been introduced. It is difficult for legislation to keep up with the pace of change, but the following section covers the main legislative acts in place at the present time.

Data Protection Act 1998

The Data Protection Act regulates how personal data is used and protects data subjects from the misuse of their personal data.

If a data user wishes to store personal data about living individuals, they must first register with the Information Commission, stating what data they want to hold, how long they intend to keep it for what they intend to do with it, and who they might pass it on to.

The data user must appoint a named data controller who ensures that the organisation complies with these principles. The data controller is an individual who is over the age of 18 and has the main responsibility for all data held.

Data subjects have the following rights:

- to see what data is being help about them (there may be a charge for this);
- to have any errors corrected
- to refuse to allow data to be processed for direct mail (sometimes called junk mail)
- to refuse to allow sensitive data (eg ethnic origins, political opinions, religious beliefs, trade union membership) to be processed
- to complain to the data protection commissioner about any abuse of the act
- to claim compensation if they have been caused damage by the misuse of the act

Getting access to your data

The act, with some exceptions, gives you the right to find out what data is held about you by organisations. This is known as the 'right of subject access'. On written request, you are entitled to be provided with a copy of all the data an organisation holds about you. This can also be done in person and you must be able to prove your identity by means of some form of identification.

Exemptions to the act

You cannot demand to see data that might affect national security or hinder police investigations.

Some data (for instance the Electoral Roll) has to be publicly available, and you cannot refuse to allow its publication.

Role of the Data Protection Commissioner

The commissioner is responsible for :

- enforcing and overseeing the Act
- raising awareness of the act and its implications
- investigating complaints.

Computer Misuse Act

Introduction

The Computer Misuse Act became law in August 1990. Under the Act unauthorised entry into ICT systems (sometimes referred to as hacking/cracking) and the introduction of viruses are made criminal offences. These are serious offences and organisations are encouraged to take action under the criminal law, but some are reluctant to do so, as it acknowledges breaches of their security.

Definition

The Act identifies three specific offences:

1 unauthorised access to computer material (that is, a program or data), even just to prove that it is possible to gain access or just 'look around'; in fact it is actually a level 1 offence to attempt to gain access to a system for which you are not authorised, even if you do not succeed.

2 unauthorised access with intent to commit or facilitate commission of further offences; for example obtaining personal data such as Internet-banking passwords, which are then used to commit fraud.

Fig. 13.6 *Using someone else's password is illegal*

3 unauthorised modification of computer material; for example, changing the account figures in a bank's computer system or introducing a computer virus to a system.

What can happen to individuals under the law

Level 1 (the basic offence) as a summary offence carries a maximum prison sentence of six months or a maximum fine of £2,000 or both.

Offences (2) and (3) are punishable with imprisonment for a term not exceeding five years, or a fine or both. These sentences clearly reflect the perceived gravity of the offence.

Example 1: Unauthorised access to computer material

This would include: using another person's **user name and password** without proper authority in order to use data or a program, reading examination papers or examination results and essentially having a look around.

An employee guesses her supervisor's password and accesses personal data about other employees just out of curiosity. This is a level 1 offence as she knows she is not authorised to view this data but has no intent to commit a further crime and does not intend to change or delete anything.

Example 2: Unauthorised access to a computer with intent to commit a further crime

This would include, for example, gaining unauthorised access to a user's credit card details and then using them to order goods fraudulently from a website.

Fig. 13.7 *Destroying another user's files is illegal*

> ### Key terms
>
> **User names** and **passwords**: most organisations use this as the basis for security of computers and networked systems. All employees have a user name and are expected to change passwords on a regular basis. The password chosen should be a mix of numbers and letters and should not be easy to guess or written down on a scrap of paper.

Example 3: Unauthorised modification of computer material

This would include: deleting another user's files; modifying system files; creating and sending of a virus although not creation on its own; or, as in the case of some adware, running code that takes up so much of the system resources that the computer fails to function properly.

Activity

Examples of possible security breaches

The following are fictitious scenarios that might occur and are examples of how some ICT systems could be compromised.

Scenario A

An office manager transmits a file to the human resources manager. The file contains payroll records that need to be protected from disclosure. A technician, who is not authorised to read the file, is able to monitor the transmission and capture a copy of the file during its transmission.

Scenario B

A network manager transmits a message to a computer under their management. The message instructs the computer to update an authorisation file to include the identities of a number of new users who can be given access to the computer. Another user intercepts the file, alters its contents to increase his own security levels, and then forwards the message to the destination computer, which accepts the message as coming from the network manager and updates the authorisation file accordingly.

Discuss the above scenarios and try to write down which ICT-related or computer-related legislation, if any, has been broken for each scenario. Suggest ways that the breaches of security should have been prevented or detected.

Action to deal with misuse

💡 *Preventive measures*

The simplest form of preventive action is training, so that all employees are perfectly clear about what their responsibilities are and what standards are expected of them. The conditions of use for computing facilities should spell out the seriousness of any misuse of ICT systems.

Computer security

Security mechanisms including the use of user names and passwords, access levels, **firewalls** and **anti-virus software** are used by organisations to try to prevent unauthorised access to their computer systems. These are known as **security services** and all organisations should build them into their ICT security plans.

A good website to check out to ensure that you are making yourself as secure as possible against security attacks is www.getsafeonline.org.

💡 Copyright, Designs and Patents Act 1988

The Copyright, Designs and Patents Act of 1988 is the current UK copyright law. This act applies to computer software as well as non-ICT-

Key terms

Security mechanism: mechanism that is designed to detect, prevent or recover from a security attack.

Firewall: acts as a barrier between the public Internet and your private computer or network and blocks threats including some viruses. A firewall is a preventive measure against external threats and is a first line of defence but must be used with care and in conjunction with other security measures to be effective.

Anti-virus software: one of the main defences against online problems from internal and external threats. It continually scans for viruses, including trojans and worms and can be set to run at particular times of the day. To be effective it must be kept up-to-date. There are many free and affordable virus checkers. If you have 15 minutes to spare now check out www.avast.com and get your own computer system checked before it is too late.

Security service: service that enhances the security of the data-processing systems and the data transfers of an organisation. The services are intended to counter security attacks, and they make use of one or more security mechanisms to provide the services.

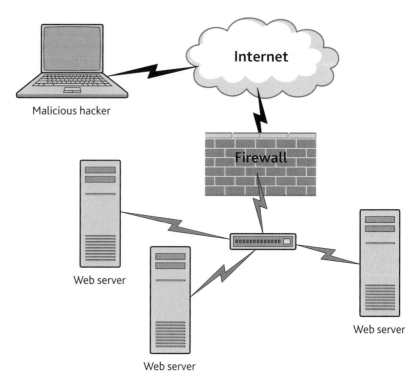

Fig. 13.8 *How a firewall works*

related media like music and gives the creator control over the ways in which their material may be used.

The law covers the actual creation rather than the idea behind it. The idea for a piece of software would not be protected, just the actual coding of the software written. Someone else is still entitled to write their own software based around the same idea, provided they do not directly copy or adapt yours to do so.

All games and software titles are covered under this act and it is a deterrent to the illegal copying of these particular formats.

When you purchase a piece of software it is the licence that you are purchasing and you do not have ownership to do as you wish. As soon as you open the packet containing the software, you are deemed to have accepted the terms of the licence.

Types of licence available:

- A single-user licence allows the user to install the software on a single machine (it sometimes also allows installation on a laptop as long as both machines are not in use at once).
- A multi-user licence agreement allows a number of installations, up to the maximum in the agreement. It may be possible to install these on a network server as long as the maximum number of concurrent users is not exceeded. That means that if you have a 25-user licence, the 26th person to log on should be denied access to the software.
- A site licence that allows any number of users within that site to use the software, but forbids its use anywhere else.

End of sub-topic questions

7 If the security measures put in place fail to keep external threats at bay, what legislation is in place to prosecute offenders?

8 Describe the measures put in place by the Data Protection Act and describe the effectiveness of the legislation.

In this section you have covered:

- the privacy of data in ICT systems
- that data has a commercial and intrinsic value
- the fact that there are both internal and external threats to an ICT system
- the difference between malpractice and crime
- the measures that can be taken to try to protect all parts of ICT systems, including networks, against threats
- the different legislation that has been introduced and the legal action that can be taken in the event of security breaches.

In this section you will cover:

- backup strategies in an ICT system
- recovery of data in an ICT system
- how often data should be backed up
- types of storage media used in backup
- responsibilities for backup and the need for continuity of service.

14.1 Backup

The previous section described some of the threats to data that could cause it to become corrupted or unavailable through theft. Given the fact that most organisations rely very heavily on their data and cannot function without it, it is vital to make sure that a backup copy is available from which data can be recovered quickly and efficiently. As the graphic in Fig. 14.2 shows, if the data is not recoverable, there is a high probability that the company will go out of business.

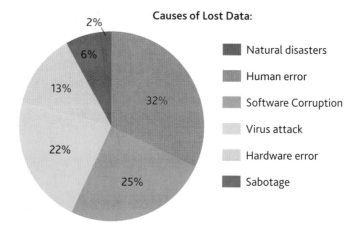

Fig. 14.1 *Causes of lost data*

Activity

A company offering backup solutions carried out a survey of medium to large size businesses who admitted to losing data in the previous year. The results are shown in the chart above.

For each of the causes, explain what could have caused the data loss or corruption and what precautions the companies could take to try to prevent the loss happening in the future.

Activity

Imagine that your school's or college's main server was damaged or stolen so that its data was no longer available.

What would be the consequences if all the files that you have stored on computer were not backed up correctly?

Think about who would be affected and the consequences of the data being irretrievable.

Write a short article expressing your thoughts about this scenario.

Fig. 14.2 *How would organisations fare if their computers failed?*

The exercise on p142 should remind you that it is not only commercial organisations that are affected if data files are lost or corrupted. As the previous section explained, there are several ways in which this can happen, including natural disasters, lack of computer security and failure of hardware and software. All these problems could cause data to be unavailable, and the time and other resources that were used to capture and process that data will have been wasted. Lost data equals loss of work time and ultimately this will cost money to rectify, retrieve or even start again from scratch.

↗ 💡 ◪ Backup strategies

Any person or organisation that stores data needs to have a backup and recovery strategy in place to make sure that it can recover any data that becomes lost or corrupted. The details of that strategy will depend on the answers to the following questions:

- What data needs to be backed up?
- How often does the data need to be backed up?
- When does the data need to be backed up?
- Which backup media will be used?
- Who will be responsible?
- Where will the data be stored?

All organisations or individuals using ICT systems will at some time need to use the backup strategy that they have in place. This might involve retrieving a single document or carrying out a much more extensive recovery such as a customer database management system with orders and financial details. The lack of a proper backup strategy

Remember

Remember the length of time it will take to restore data is dependent on the backup types that are chosen and the media on which the data is stored.

could cause an organisation serious difficulties and possibly put them out of business.

In Section 5 we saw that the health and safety risks within an organisation could be tackled via the process of risk assessment. The same process can be used to develop a backup strategy. The person responsible for backup needs to assess what risks apply to the data and how likely it is that the hazards creating those risks will take place. They then need to think about what the effect would be on the organisation if the event occurred. This will obviously vary depending on the extent to which the organisation relies on its data. For some organisations their ICT system is mission critical. That means they cannot operate without it. Banks, airlines, insurance companies and hospitals are some obvious examples, but many shops and supermarkets would come into the same category because their operations depend so heavily on their EPOS systems.

For many organisations it is also critical that they can recover quickly, as they could be losing hundreds of thousands of pounds for every minute their systems are inoperable. Most private individuals would be unhappy about losing data, and may incur financial costs through it, but the speed of recovery is less likely to be a major issue for them. Once the consequences of data loss have been established through the risk assessment, the individual or organisation has to decide on a financial budget to be spent on backup and recovery to reduce their risks to an acceptable level.

What data needs to be backed up?

The amount of data that needs to be backed up will affect many of the decisions that need to be made. This will be dependent on the size of the organisation and the value that the data has for the organisation.

Full backup

As suggested by the term 'full backup', all data that is stored in your files or folders that you wish to back up will be saved. This means that they can be restored quickly if something goes wrong with your ICT system. If there was unlimited time and resources this would be the most sensible form of backup for most organisations. A full backup can take a long time, depending on the quantity of data to be backed up. This is the reason that many organisations only schedule a weekly or even monthly full backup. Data is certainly better protected if a full backup has taken place. However, as Section 13 suggests, there is a significant security issue as each full backup contains an entire copy of the data. If the backup media were to be illegally accessed or stolen, the hacker or thief would then have access to an entire copy of the organisation's data.

Worked example

Full backup

An example of a school with 300 students with 1GB of user data being backed up using a compressed LTO tape with capacity 200/400GB. It would take approximately four and a half hours to back up and verify 200GB of data which would include operating and user files, which is very fast compared to older types of tape and may mean an overnight backup is possible. More detail about the technology of the tape itself can be found by looking up LTO tape at www.tech-faq.com.

Imagine the length of time that it would take to back up the data stored by a large bank or other commercial organisation – possibly even your own school or college if there are large numbers of people using the ICT system.

If full backups are not feasible, there are other alternatives.

Differential backup

As the word differential suggests, only data that is different since the last full backup will be saved. This reduces the time it takes to restore data because it only uses the previous full and differential backups. Sometimes, however, if differential backups are performed too many times the size of the backup can actually become larger than the full backup. The data to be backed up is selected automatically by the backup software that is being used by the organisation. This type of backup is slower than an incremental backup. Only the two container files (full and differential) are needed but they may contain files that have already been included in the recent differential backup and have not actually been modified.

Incremental backup

Incremental backups save all of the files that have changed since the last backup, whether that was a full backup, differential or, indeed, incremental.

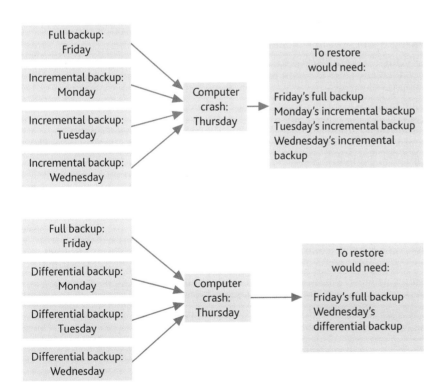

Fig. 14.3 *Restore procedures needed for incremental and differential backups*

The diagrams clearly show that the use of the differential backup saves time during the restore procedure by only needing the Friday full backup and the Wednesday differential. Any data entered on Thursday would be lost in either of these cases.

It is the fastest way to back up, but restore jobs can take a long time to perform because of the processing involved. This is certainly a quicker method of backup than always running full backups as only files that have changed are included. Again, the software automatically chooses the files that have changed since the last full backup. The advantage of an incremental backup is that it takes the least time to complete, but this advantage is offset by increased restore times. This is because the last full backup has to be used during the operation as well as all of the incremental backups taken in that time period.

Table 14.1 *Summary table of backup types and benefits and limitations of each*

Type of backup	Time taken to perform backup	Restore time required for backup	Storage space required
FULL	A long process as all data is backed up	A very quick method of restore	Large amounts of storage space required
DIFFERENTIAL	More than incremental but can be quicker than a full backup	Less than incremental but takes longer than a full backup	Less storage space than a full backup but more than an incremental
INCREMENTAL	The least time taken of the three methods	The slowest restore speed of the three methods	Storage space is the lowest of the three methods

How often should data be backed up?

The answer to this question is that it depends on how often the data changes and how much data the organisation is prepared to lose. In any backup strategy, there is a possibility of losing any data that changes between the time the data becomes corrupt and the time of the last backup. For instance, if the data is backed up every night, there is a danger of losing a day's data if, for example, a hard drive fails.

The ideal situation is for data to be backed up as soon as it changes, and for that reason, most server-based systems have RAID drives that save the data onto several drives at the same time in a process called 'mirroring'. That means that if one drive fails, the next one takes over and there is no loss of data. A new drive can be hot swapped to replace the corrupted one and so the server does not need to be switched off and the service remains continuous. This system is essential if data is changing rapidly and no data loss is acceptable. Indeed, for mission-critical servers the data may also be copied to a second server in a different location. It is also the best solution if the computers are in use for 24 hours a day and there is no time at which a backup can conveniently be taken. Many organisations view their database management systems as mission critical and see any disruption in service as being disastrous in terms of customer satisfaction.

When does the data need to be backed up?

Many systems back their data up overnight when the data files are not in use. Sometimes this is in addition to the mirrored drives, sometimes this is the only backup. Files cannot normally be backed up when they are in use, so the backup is scheduled to start during the evening and continue overnight. If this is the only backup taken, there is a possibility that a full day of new data may be lost.

Program and system files might not change as frequently as data files, and so they might only be backed up when they are changed.

Computers used for personal use also need to have any important data backed up, but for many users, a weekly backup may be enough.

How should the data be backed up?

As explained above, it is possible to do a full, incremental or differential backup, but it may also be necessary to mix these methods, taking a full backup every so often. Decisions need to be made about how long removable backup media should be kept before being overwritten. The classic backup strategy of 'grandfather, father, son' (i.e. 3 copies) is probably less common now than a daily backup (i.e. 5 or 7 copies). The tapes or other media need to be labelled and stored logically so that the correct tape in sequence is inserted at the correct time.

As part of the backup strategy, it is most important to check that the backed-up data has been recorded properly and is actually accessible should it be needed. The recovery procedure needs to be tested to make sure that the organisation can return to normal operations within the scheduled time period. This may involve reserving equipment and office space that could be used to move operations to in case of a disaster.

Types of storage media used in backup

Section 3 gives details of storage media and devices, but it is still useful to consider which of them are most suitable for backup in a given situation.

Magnetic tape

The most commonly used medium for storing large quantities of data and for archiving has historically been magnetic tape. It has a high capacity and is fairly inexpensive when compared to hard disks, although prices have become closer in recent years. Different formats exist and some are specific to a particular market like a mainframe or even different brands of personal computer. Access is sequential and this makes it quite a laborious process to find particular files or folders. On the other hand the time taken to write or read data on a continuous basis can be fast. As tape drives have developed they can be faster than some hard disks and have remained the main backup choice for many organisations when backing up large amounts of data.

Hard disks

Hard disks have become ever more affordable and now compete with magnetic tape for the storage of large amounts of data. The hard disk has low access times, high capacity and is fairly easy to use. You will probably be familiar with hard disks being connected externally via different types of interface including USB and FireWire.

Optical disc

The other medium that you will have become familiar with will be recordable CDs. Although the disc capacity of around 700 MB makes them really only suitable for use at home or in small business use, the advantage of this medium is that rather than being accessed in sequence, data can be accessed directly and this means recovery times can be lowered. Most computers have rewritable CD drives and it means there is no need for expensive extras to allow backup to take place. This cost saving is also reflected in the fact that recordable CDs are readily available at a low cost in comparison to other types of backup media. As prices of optical disks fall, recordable DVDs and the DVD recorders

Fig. 14.4 *Scott Crawford examines a robotic arm inside 'Happy', a computer storage device at the CIA headquarters, Virginia, USA. The arm is used to move 5,900 magnetic tapes holding 1.2 million megabytes of information.*

are a popular option, with a much larger storage space of around 4.7 GB. New technologies like HD-DVDs and Blu-ray are allowing for increased storage space, although the hardware needed is still prohibitive in terms of cost. No doubt they will be an option for large-scale data storage for many organisations as costs fall in the future.

Remote backup service

Broadband and other means of high-speed Internet access have meant that online backup is becoming a popular option for many companies. There is a reduction in the risk that natural disasters, fire or even terrorist attack can cause. This is because all the organisation's data is backed up in an off-site location. This option does, however, require very high-speed Internet access as it will always be slower to back up large amounts of data from a remote server than from a locally accessible storage device. There are also the security risks of trusting a third party to look after what may be very valuable and often sensitive data.

■ 14.2 Recovery

■ Responsibilities for backup and recovery

It may be that because you are used to logging on to a network with a server you very rarely think about the backup that is actually occurring as this is the responsibility of the network manager. However, the backup of data is everyone's responsibility. If you are working on a standalone computer or a laptop then it is your responsibility to ensure that your PC and, more importantly, the data stored on it are adequately protected.

A network manager takes responsibility for backup based upon the policies that have been set out in the company's backup and recovery procedures. A good disaster recovery plan is essential and will minimise the impact that any disaster that involves the potential loss of data will have on the business.

A specific person needs to be designated to look after the backup procedure, changing tapes when necessary and storing them appropriately. A second person needs to be in place in case the first person is ill or otherwise unavailable.

■ Where is valuable data stored?

Having taken a lot of time and money to make a backup it would now be prudent to ensure that it is stored somewhere safe and away from the original PC or server. This can often be at a remote base or in another part of the organisation in a fire- (and flood-) proof safe. In some organisations the person responsible for backing up simply takes the previous tape home overnight. The storage location needs to be secure, because the theft of backup media could well hand a complete set of organisational data over to a thief.

■ Need for continuity of service

In any business that uses ICT systems there is a need to ensure that services are not disturbed for too long because of an interruption in the ICT network. Sometimes this requires immediate action if, for example, they provide online services such as online insurance

AQA **Examiner's tip**

Be careful about what media types you quote in questions about backup: floppy discs do not hold enough data to back up modern systems; flash memory is too vulnerable to damage as it could be dropped and the files it holds may become corrupt; CD-ROMs are read-only, so cannot be used to back anything up.

companies who have no income source if their website is not operational. It is still the case in some organisations that important servers are stored in basements or in the corner of an office with no uninterruptible power supply (UPS) and little means of keeping them cool. Organisations should put in place a policy to ensure that servers are situated in the correct location and all appropriate backup and security measures are in place to ensure the continuity of service is as reliable as is possible. This may be expensive in the short term but the security of the network and the data stored must be seen as a priority for any business to ensure that they can continue to trade without interruptions.

Example

BCP continuity of service after disaster strikes

Business organisations do realise that continuity of service is vital. This is certainly shown in a survey of 1,257 managers that warned more comprehensive planning for continuity of service is required if for any reason their ICT system were to fail.

In the Business Continuity Management Institute's eighth report on Business Continuity Management since 1999 it was revealed that many UK organisations are paying lip service to the importance of planning for disaster, but are actually failing to make business resilience a reality. The number of managers whose organisations actually have a business continuity plan (BCP) covering critical areas like ICT is around 48 per cent. This is a worrying trend and it is often only after repeated problems or external pressure from government or indeed loss of business that proper planning is put in place.

(*Source*: Based on Business Continuity Management (March 2007), **Author:** Patrick Woodman)

From the statistics it can be seen that ignoring proper backup and security strategies can have a devastating effect on all organisations using ICT systems. Each year, one in five businesses suffers a major disruption in their services. With this in mind it would be advisable for all businesses that are reliant on ICT systems to put in place what is often referred to as disaster recovery planning (DRP). This should mean that the business can:

- Resume trading quickly by ensuring ICT services are back online as soon as possible.
- Give customers, investors and trading partners confidence in the reliability of the company.
- Retain customers who might change companies if there is a loss in trading time.

Case study: Fulcrum Pharma

Disaster recovery plan used during the Buncefield fuel depot fire

In 2005 Fulcrum Pharma a drug development services company used what is called a Wide Area File Services (WAFS) based disaster recovery plan when the offices that they were moving into were

Did you know?

Statistics gathered by the London Chamber of Commerce show that:

- 90 per cent of businesses that lose data from a disaster are forced to close within two years of the disaster.
- 80 per cent of businesses without a well-structured recovery plan are forced to close within 12 months of a flood or fire.
- 43 per cent of companies experiencing disasters never recover.
- 50 per cent of companies experiencing a **computer outage** will be forced to shut within five years.

Key terms

Computer outage: when an organisation's computer system is interrupted by some form of disaster including power cuts, fire, flood and terrorist attack.

affected by the Buncefield fire. A specialist company called Availl had provided a solution that collected common data from all of the international offices and replicated it across the network to a disaster recovery site based in London. Some copies were also stored in the USA.

'People talk about it being a disaster but it didn't really affect our business. We were about to move to an office in the Buncefield area, and had already installed four servers there, but the Availl network let us carry on working as though nothing had happened', said Fulcrum IT manager Jason Hamlett.

Fulcrum had also deployed a number of other routines for disaster recovery in its regional branch offices, including Veritas software for disk-based backups which are then replicated back to the central office using WAFS. In addition to that is a central document management system, which backs up some 120 GB of data to disk then replicates it across the globe.

'We cover ourselves by sending the data to both our US office and our head office, which is in the same location as the disaster recovery suite hosted in central London', says Hamlett.

After the fire, almost a third of Fulcrum's staff were forced to stay away from the office or work from home. The Availl WAFS commercial solution helped out by allowing some of them to access the data replicated to the US offices.

'The nature of the backup service we run puts a lot of stress on the disaster recovery site, so that this becomes a target in itself. We get around this by spreading backups across different sites using WAFS, so we can lose two out of three and still remain operational', said Hamlett. 'Backing up to tape and storing those tapes off-site still goes on in both the UK and US offices, however; that is largely a regulatory requirement and is unlikely ever to change.'

Fulcrum spent more than £100,000 on building the Availl WAFS solution and providing assistance with tape backups. Hamlett says that although he cannot identify any clear return on investment from having done this, at least both he and the finance director can sleep soundly at night.

(*Source*: IT Week)

Case study: Wildfowl and Wetlands Trust

More efficient data backups from multiple sites

In 2004 Ian Wood, head of IT at the Wildfowl and Wetlands Trust (WWT), a registered international conservation charity, was running localised backups on individual servers at each of the organisation's offices spread across England, Scotland, Northern Ireland and Wales.

The trust wanted to save money by consolidating e-mail and file servers, and run more efficient backups that did not duplicate the same data at multiple sites, but found that its WAN capacity was not up to the job.

'We wanted to provide a single network, bring all the servers back into our headquarters, hold all the data there and have everybody access it from the other offices', says Wood.

'Because the speed of the WAN wasn't appropriate, each centre became an island of data. There was a lot of data duplication, and we didn't know if it was good duplication or not.'

By installing a WAN optimisation device at its central office, all data backups are now performed remotely but transmitted to the central office for storage. This makes the backups much easier to control and verify, while restores are quicker to perform if data is lost at one or more branch offices.

Better WAN response times mean users can also save their data over the network much more frequently, without fear of depriving other applications of the bandwidth they need.

As a charity, return on investment was very important to the WWT, and Wood estimates that WAN optimisation is saving the organisation about £15,000 to £20,000 per year.

John Malachy, *Computing*, 2 Nov 2006

Student group activity

Make up a recovery plan for all of the essential data and information that an organisation has. This can be any organisation and it may be your school/college, a business that you have a link with or a global organisation that you are familiar with.

Take into account:

- method
- timing
- storage capacity
- value of data
- where backup will be stored
- how it will be accessed in an emergency
- development of a continuity plan
- adding more comprehensive security and access methods to your buildings
- provisioning resilient power for your servers
- provisioning resilient methods for you to access your data
- storing your data offsite.

Take time to back up all of the data that you have on the various ICT systems that you use. Check that all of your AS files are being backed up on a server and make copies of other files that are not being stored on your school college network. Make sure that you label and date the backups and store them in an appropriate place away from the original data. You may even want to invest in some form of storage that protects against fire and flood.

✔ *In this section you have covered:*

- the need for systematic backup procedures to be in place
- the various backup strategy options available and the use for each
- the what, when, where and who of backing up
- how organisations make decisions about the data that will be backed up
- the distinction between full, incremental and differential backups
- that there are different media that can store backups and online backups are also available
- the factors that influence how often backups should be made
- the need to decide who is responsible for the backups
- the storage options for storing backup media
- the reasons why continuity of service is important
- what is in a disaster recovery plan.

15 Uses of ICT systems

In this section you will cover:

- what can be provided by the use of ICT

- whether the use of ICT systems is always appropriate

- the different types of processing used in ICT systems.

15.1 What ICT can provide

As discussed in previous sections the use of ICT and ICT systems by organisations has increased significantly over the past few years and will continue to do so in a very rapidly changing environment. There are many reasons for this increase and the resulting use of ICT to store and process data and to search for information has to be understood against this background.

> Three quarters of the 'new or significantly improved internal processes' introduced by EU firms in 2004 were directly related to ICT.
>
> *Source: European e-Business Report 2005*

Fast, repetitive processing

Probably the biggest single reason for using computers is because they can perform calculations very quickly. The ability to process repetitive calculations at high speed is particularly useful in situations where large volumes of data and complex sets of variables are involved. Supercomputers were used to model and map human DNA in the Human Genome Project but lots of ordinary applications such as record keeping and financial management also benefit from the fast processing speeds of more modest computers.

The use of ICT in the making of animations and other films has allowed the production of films which would have been impossible, or at the very least difficult, such as *The Lord of the Rings*. The computer graphics that were used in the production of the film were made possible by the advances that have been made in computer technology and ICT systems.

Vast storage capacity

The ability to store data electronically means that records and documents can be kept in a much smaller physical space than would otherwise be necessary. These records can then be made available to other interested parties without making paper-based copies because they can form part of a shared database or can be attached to an e-mail and sent electronically. A good example would be census records. Originally these were collected on paper and stored in one central location. There are a huge number of these records, and they all take up space. As technology developed, copies were made and stored in lots of locations, so they took up lots of space in many different locations. Then they were stored on microfilm, so took up less space but still had to be stored in many locations. Now census data is entered into a computer system as it is collected and old census records have also been transcribed into computers. Now the records can be stored in one place but accessed from anywhere, although they are not available publicly until 100 years after they were collected.

Improved search facilities

Modern ICT systems give users the facility to search and combine data in many different ways that otherwise would be impossible.

Fig. 15.1 *Doctor can use expert systems to aid diagnostics.*

The use of ICT systems allows for the processing of large amounts of data in a very short time. Doctors, for example, can find information on patients and possibly even look up diagnoses on an expert system and receive answers to questions in a much shorter time than would be possible without the use of ICT. In the case of the census data, one major benefit is that the electronic data can be searched quickly by researchers to find results that could previously have taken months or even years because the original records were indexed by address and so it was impossible to do a search for a particular name.

The setting up of a national DNA database and the ability to search the vast quantity of records it holds has made a huge impact on the detection rate of crimes.

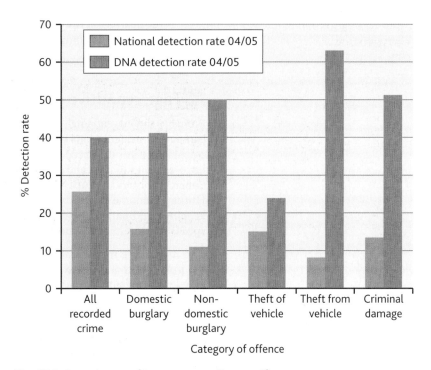

Fig. 15.2 *Detection rates (Source: www.parliament.uk)*

Improved presentation of information

The use of multimedia technology means that information can be presented in a much wider variety of ways than was previously available. Consider the output of news information by television stations. They can use animations and computer-generated special effects to help them explain complex problems such as election forecasting, economic growth, or even the weather. They can transmit pictures and sounds via a satellite live from a war zone where children are starving, to try to involve the public more directly with the plight of such children. News programmes can be stored as podcasts so that viewers can download them to their PDA, then watch and listen on the train on their way to work. Electronic voting systems enable viewers to join in with quizzes and surveys by pressing the red button on their digital TV, the results of which are available almost instantly. TV stations also upload the news to their websites, and so make it available 24 hours a day. The websites have, to some extent, replaced teletext, as they can make much better use of graphics and search facilities.

End of sub-topic questions

1 Many supermarkets now use EPOS systems at their checkouts. Explain the advantages of an EPOS system over a manual till system, and explain which of the factors discussed above have made EPOS systems possible.

2 Educational material is today available in many different formats. Describe three different ways such material can be presented, and discuss the advantages and disadvantages of each of them.

Improved accessibility of information and services

As some of the examples above have indicated, the growth of database management systems, spreadsheets and online information services has made information and services much more accessible to many individuals and organisations than they were previously.

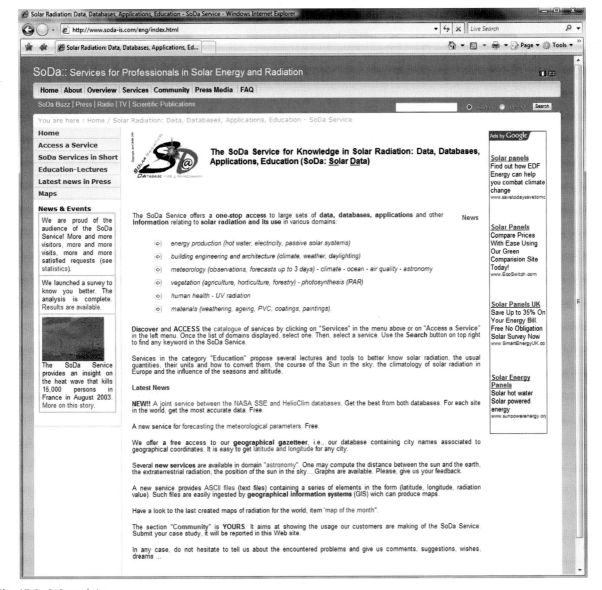

Fig. 15.3 *SoDa website*

■ Case study – new information accessibility from the Internet

Solar radiation from SoDa

In the modern digital world there is an amazing amount of information available to help people in all sorts of situations. It is amazing to think that we can now find out instantly about the solar radiation in Brighton in August 1960 or, indeed, in Rome. The system called SoDa is a new technology developed by oncologists that can help them see how much exposure their patients have had to the sun and therefore provide better advice on courses of treatment. This shows that access to information can help improvement of service.

Lucien Wald, Head of the SoDa project, gave this example that can show how it could be used: 'Imagine you live in Denmark and you're about to spend your holiday in Southern Italy where solar radiation is extremely strong. With a few clicks on SoDa, your oncologist will be able to find the types of UV A and B radiation you'll be the most exposed to, and on which beaches at certain times. Armed with this information, we can limit your risk of developing cancer.'

The ICT system is easy to use as the user connects to the website www.soda-is.com and locates a city on the world map. Within a short period of time information about the solar radiation in a particular city will be provided and decisions can be made.

The above is just one example of how a database can be accessed to provide the appropriate information from a huge dataset, improving access to information.

Many organisations, including radio stations and concert or festival organisations, use web cams, like the one in Fig. 15.4 on p158 to encourage people to first view what is going on and, ultimately, try to get them to come and visit.

Weather forecasters in holiday resorts and especially ski resorts often use this as a technique to encourage holidaymakers to come and visit. This means that information is available 24 hours a day 7 days a week. Information is available on many different subjects and there is now less need to have to wait for traditional information centres like libraries and tourist information centres to be open to find out about a destination. This can improve the service available to people using them as long as it is in an appropriate manner.

Improved communication now enables us to use web blogs, podcasts, chat rooms, messaging services and other interactive services where information is communicated between individuals and also between organisations.

■ Activity

Check out some web cams and see if you think they would actually attract you to go to a place or do they just provide the information that they have been set up for? Can you think of a destination that would benefit from a web cam but doesn't currently have one?

Fig. 15.4 *Capital City Centre web cam*

Improved security of data and processes

All data and processes that take place in ICT systems have to be secure. When the appropriate techniques and software are chosen this can ensure that any processing that takes place within an ICT system is as secure as possible, otherwise it would not be the correct way of producing the information from the system. This security is likely to be provided by a combination of the steps that we have already looked at in Section 13.

15.2 Is the use of ICT systems always appropriate?

Is ICT always the best solution? Of course not. There are many situations where ICT will not be the most appropriate way of handling a problem.

Limitations in what ICT systems can be used for

It is in the very nature of the ICT industry to push the boundaries of what can be achieved. The amount of technology that we take for granted in a mobile phone today would have taken a whole suite of computers to achieve 30 years ago. However, ICT systems do have limitations and it is estimated about 75 per cent of large ICT projects fail to achieve what they set out to, or are brought in late or over budget. It is very difficult when starting out on something genuinely innovative, because there is the possibility of failure, and the many failed ICT projects are testament to this fact.

ICT systems have cost limitations: it may be more expensive to use ICT to solve a problem than it would to do it in another way.

There are still many things that human beings do better than computers, such as understanding speech and recognising faces. There is an enormous amount of research going on to make computers better at each of those things but, as yet, people still have the upper hand. Human beings use opinion, for example, within forecasting systems – this does not always translate well into an ICT system.

There is also the possibility that when a student watches a podcast on a topic being covered they may be able to watch it over and over again but still not understand. The limitation in this case is that there is no teacher to ask to explain the topic in more detail to aid understanding.

ICT systems have limitations in the information that they produce

As we have seen in previous sections, the quality of the information produced by a computer system is only as good as the data put into it, and not all input errors can be picked up by validation. The output information is also controlled by the processing that the computer carries out, and this processing is generally specified by human beings based on a set of rules. If those rules are incorrect or they are not replicated exactly by the programming code, the information will be incorrect too. The danger of computer systems is that somehow the output they produce tends to look extremely convincing and it is not always obvious that there is a problem. New systems should always be tested, but as computer systems can be extremely complex, it is almost impossible to test every single aspect of them, and errors may not be spotted.

ICT cannot model opinions so the information produced is limited. ICT cannot replicate people's opinions, it can only put them into categories; for example, value judgements may have to be coded from 1 to 10.

If we look at digital output, for example, sound is sampled and does not have the same gradation as it had when it was analogue.

Appropriateness of solutions

There may be times when ICT does not provide the best solution in a particular set of circumstances. If the amount of data to be handled is very small, it may take longer to set up a spreadsheet or database than produce the information by hand with a pencil and calculator. There are times when the personal touch is needed. Whilst many people would be happy to use NHS Direct online for advice about minor injuries or illnesses, most people would prefer to talk to a real doctor about a serious problem.

End of sub-topic questions

3 State some of the security issues that may arise because of the easy accessibility of information.

4 Describe some of the issues that arise through consumers using information from websites and not other sources.

5 State some of the limitations of the use of ICT systems.

15.3 Types of processing

There are three main types of processing that are used in ICT systems and each is used under different circumstances depending on the processing taking place and the availability and cost of the processing.

Batch

In modern ICT systems in the digital world a batch job is where data is collected together in a group or batch before processing takes place. Transaction files store jobs in queues until the computer system is ready to start processing. When the job is run, the data held in the transaction file is used to update the master file. The master file is stored on disk and stays the same until any updating takes place by a new transaction file. While running the program there is no interaction between computer and user. This allows for overnight jobs to be completed using spare capacity in the ICT system. Backing up is fairly simple and can be done after each new job is run.

Examples _____

A payroll system – all the wages are calculated and the payslips are output.

Power supply bills for customers – readings are grouped together in a batch and then processed when all of the readings have been taken. This may take place every evening and produce the final bill for customers at the end of a given time period. The user at this point has no interaction and the processing and output are done automatically by the ICT system.

Batch processing is best suited to regular jobs that happen at scheduled times and involve large quantities of data, such as the examples given. Because of the time available, batch processing tends to have strong error-checking features built in, and so the information produced tends to be extremely accurate. It tends to use fewer system resources than interactive processing, as it does not need a live communication link between the computer and a user for most of the time in the way that interactive processing does.

Interactive

In this type of processing there is interaction between the ICT system and the user. The user reacts to prompts from the computer and the computer uses these prompts to process data. Many computer systems in the modern world work this way.

Example _____

A student queries their record in the college library database to see if they have exceeded the maximum number of books they can take out. The reply comes up on screen immediately which means they know whether or not they can take out another book.

As can be seen from the above example the interaction occurs in real time and the input–process–output is controlled by the user:

■ The computer is available to receive the input from the user.

■ The data is processed at the time it is input and output is also immediate.

■ Transaction processing

Transaction processing allows many users to access and update a system at apparently the same time. Each transaction must be completed before the next transaction is begun.

The main aim of a transaction processing system is to be able to work quickly with a large amount of different transactions taking place, sometimes from many different users.

You or your family may be familiar with online transaction processing systems; for example, a travel booking system or when purchasing cinema tickets using the ICT booking system.

Example _____

Travel enquiries

Passengers may make enquiries at travel agents anywhere in the world to find out if a seat is free on any of the flights operated by any airline. Passengers require immediate up-to-date information. The travel agent can make online contact with the main travel company, giving the agent

■ Remember

Many systems use both interactive and transaction processing, but no systems use interactive and batch processing.

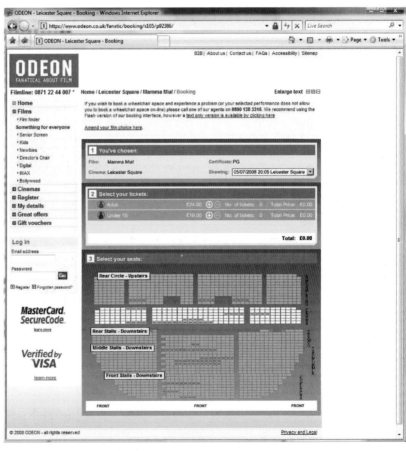

Fig. 15.5 *Cinema ticket booking – transaction processing*

and the customer access to the flight information and booking file held on the main computer.

The main computer should support multi-access, as there may be many travel agents wanting to make enquiries at the same time. The information requested can be displayed instantaneously and will be kept up to date while displayed on the screen.

Booking a seat

The customer may decide to book a seat on a flight. The travel agent books the flight online. Once a seat has been booked the flight information file must be updated immediately, so that further enquiries show the seat as already booked. When the flight information and booking file is being accessed to book a flight, to avoid double booking, all other attempts to book the seat must be locked out. Tickets for booked seats may be printed out on the spot or may be sent to customers at a later date. Payment may also be made via the online link using a credit card. There should also be a facility for cancellation and refund of payments using the online link.

End of sub-topic questions

6 Identify two areas in which organisations might make use of batch processing.

7 Describe in your own words interactive processing and give an example of where it might be used.

8 Identify an organisation that would not be able to stay in business without the use of transaction processing on a daily basis.

✔ *In this section you have covered:*

- the main reason for ICT systems being popular in organisations is because of the fact that they are good at processing data quickly
- ICT systems have a vast storage capacity compared to other business methods
- ICT systems give improved search facilities for an organisation
- presentation looks more professional and access to information is much easier and allows for easy access to daily and unusual information
- the limitations of ICT systems and understanding where a particular type of ICT system is appropriate
- what batch, interactive and transaction processing are.

In this section you will learn:

- the factors affecting the use of ICT systems

- the influence of these factors on how ICT systems are chosen and used

- the consequences of the use of ICT on individuals

- the consequences of the use of ICT on society.

16.1 Factors influencing the use of ICT systems

Ever since the introduction of microcomputers in the late 1970s, computers have become an important part of daily life for individuals and organisations. Computers are vital in communications, education, government, medicine, industry and most businesses. If you have a job in a supermarket you are more than likely to use some form of ICT such as the bar code system on the till or during stock-taking on the shelves. If you want some money you will visit an ATM to withdraw cash or even top up your mobile phone. If you communicate with friends you might use e-mail or instant messaging to keep in touch. If you want tickets for a holiday or to make a concert booking you will probably do this through an online booking system. In many of these situations you may not even see the ICT system, as often they are working in the background and we take the fact that they are being used for granted. As ICT systems become more affordable and powerful, we as individuals, and society as a whole, are becoming increasingly dependent on them.

Activity

'I couldn't run my life without using my computer.'

'Society as a whole is becoming too dependent on computers.'

Discuss these statements with your group. Do you agree or disagree?

Try to think of all the situations where ICT is used in your daily life as well as the lives of people that you come into contact with at home, school or in the workplace.

Cultural

ICT systems change the way that we work which has an influence on the way individuals interact and allows for the breakdown of the traditional culture of the workplace. ICT can certainly improve the speed and amount of work that can be achieved but does mean that the culture of work and loyalty to a particular firm and organisation can break down. Some jobs lack the personal contact that employment used to offer: customers bank online and use ATMs rather than go into a bank and speak to a real person; teleworking means that more people can work from home, but also means that friendships with colleagues and loyalty to a largely unseen company may suffer. Conversely in some areas of work, online communities mean that friendships can develop worldwide.

In terms of cultural material such as art and music, many people feel that sites such as YouTube and MySpace have made it possible for lots of people to share their music, pictures and poetry with an international audience, and in this way society's traditional view of culture is changing.

Fig. 16.1 *YouTube, a popular video-sharing website*

Activity

The cultures of remote communities are changing because of access to the Internet.

Research and discuss.

Economic

There is no doubt that keeping up to date with ICT equipment is an expensive business for most organisations, as technology changes so rapidly. Investing in new ICT systems can mean that the organisations can work more efficiently, perhaps reducing costs as they need fewer staff and less office space than they would have done without the computer equipment. In many economic areas, such as retail markets, failure to embrace new technology is likely to render a business uncompetitive and make it difficult for it to exist at all. Few major retailers would consider not having a website or not using **EFTPOS** at their checkouts. In fact, many retailers have ceased to accept cheques, making card payment the only alternative to hard cash.

Key terms

EFTPOS: technology that enables instant, automatic payment directly from the customer's bank account when a debit card is used.

163

The financial industries make huge use of computer technology, whether stock market trading for millions of pounds or a customer drawing cash from an ATM for a night out in town. Over-reliance on technology could have a devastating effect on whole economies. For example, over 20 years ago, on 19 October 1987, a large fall in the American stock market occurred because of computers programmed to trade shares automatically.

■ Environmental

The green movement has become an important part of ICT planning in organisations and plays an important part in the decision-making process. The paperless office may not yet be a reality but the use of resources in the most environmentally effective manner has certainly become an important consideration in any decision about the use of ICT. Teleworking can reduce the number of journeys employees make to and from work, and videoconferencing can reduce an organisation's carbon footprint by allowing meetings to take place between people anywhere in the world without them leaving home.

Fig. 16.2 *Recycling ICT items is becoming an increasingly important issue*

On the negative side, more work needs to be done in the field of recycling unwanted equipment. With some printers now costing very little more than a set of print cartridges, it has become uneconomical to repair equipment, and it just tends to be thrown away. Even with initiatives like the EC Directive on Waste Electrical and Electronic Equipment (WEEE) (www.dti.gov.uk/innovation/sustainability/) many environmentalists now feel that ICT equipment should be reused by donating it to projects in developing countries or even to local projects in the UK.

Think!

The new three Rs mean a greener use of ICT:

- ▨ **Reduce** the amount of paper, ink and other consumables that you use.
- ▨ **Reuse** rather than just throw away computers, printers and other hardware or donate to suitable projects around the globe.
- ▨ **Recycle** appropriately via the approved schemes under the WEEE directive, which can often be done free of charge, ensuring that all important data, files and folders are removed from the ICT system before recycling.

(Based on an idea in *IT Week*, 10 September 2007, Vol. 10, No. 35)

■ Activity

Design an environmental policy for your own use of ICT systems both in the home and in any other areas of life where you use ICT. Ensure that it takes into account the need for less to be consumed as well as the need for data protection and security of any data that you have stored. Try to become more environmentally aware about your use of ICT and maybe set up good practices that others might follow which ultimately might reduce the overall carbon footprint. Ask yourself:

- ▨ What could I use less of?
- ▨ What could I reuse?
- ▨ What could I recycle?

Ethical

All individuals using ICT must look at the ethics behind what they are using ICT systems for; even if it is legal it may be against the ethics of the organisation. One area of concern involves the wasting of company time by searching the Internet for non-work-related material or sending personal e-mails, which would go against the company ICT code of practice. This can bring in ethical issues for the company such as whether they have the right to read e-mails sent to and from their employees. Many companies regularly audit Internet use in their organisations to try to make sure that their employees are using the web appropriately and not downloading inappropriate material.

Use of the Internet produces all sorts of moral and ethical dilemmas, as it is largely unregulated. Because anyone can post information on the World Wide Web, websites, including those that display photographs of children being bullied, provide information that most people would feel should not be displayed. Should these sites be policed? If so by whom? Who should have the power of censorship? Does anyone have the right to tell people what they can and can't see? Laws are different in different countries. Sites that may be legal and acceptable in their own country may be considered neither by people in another country. Some governments try very hard to regulate what content is allowed into their country by controlling what search engines are allowed to deliver. For example, many US states have made serious efforts to restrict online gambling sites. Do they have the right to do that? The issues are endless, and the answers are largely down to personal opinion and individual conscience.

Activity

Discuss these issues with others in your group or you may even want to open this discussion out to a wider audience in your school or college. It might be interesting to gauge the opinions of people from a cross-section of disciplines as well as different age groups.

Another aspect you could consider is how access to ICT might affect education and career opportunities. The gap between those with adequate access and those without is referred to as the 'digital divide'.

It is generally agreed that computers can be important educational tools. Is it fair then that some children from poorer households have no access to the Internet or even a computer at home? Does that put them at an educational disadvantage? If it does, how much more at a disadvantage are children from developing countries who have no computer access at all, and possibly no electricity to power one.

The One Laptop per Child project (www.laptop.org) aims to provide children in developing countries with a laptop computer at a cost of less than $100, and the charity is funded by donations. The laptops are robust and powered by the use of a hand crank. One scheme due to be trialled is the 'buy one give one' scheme, where for $399, one laptop is sent to the donor's own child and one to a needy child abroad.

Legal

All decisions on the use of ICT systems by individuals or organisations will be influenced by legal considerations. You have already looked at some

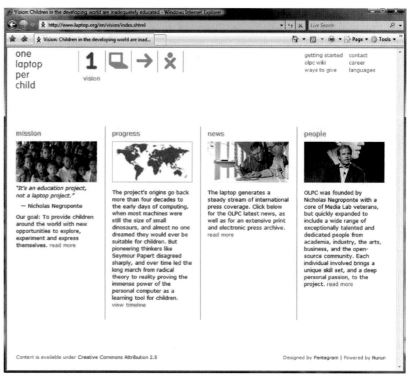

Fig. 16.3 *One Laptop per Child*

of these legal aspects in detail in Section 13. The main consideration for any organisation is to ensure that they follow all of the laws that govern the use of ICT and allow for that in their budgets. They must also ensure that procedures are in place and that adequate training has been given to staff. The Data Protection Act, for instance, demands security of data and staff members need to be trained to implement the act, and carry out such tasks as responding to data users who request a copy of their data.

For example, if a company sells goods via the Internet store, security precautions need to be in place for online financial transactions, and so the setting up and running of such a website will cost considerably more than one that just displays goods. Small companies often get round this by using an intermediate banking service such as PayPal.

Social

Teleworking, where employers or contractors work away from the office environment, has become a popular use of modern ICT systems in the digital world. This can save on some of the costs of overheads for the employer and allows some flexibility in work practice for the employee. Teleworkers are able to work at times that they find most suitable and can work around the commitments they have in the home. The disadvantage could be that teleworkers can become isolated and may not feel as though they are part of the workforce.

AQA Examiner's tip

A good way of preparing for questions about the uses of ICT is to become aware of ICT developments in the newspapers, on TV or on technology websites. The information is up to date and interesting and so you are likely to recall it when you need to.

Activity

Remember teleworking is only one use of ICT that has a social effect. Do some research and list some other areas where the use of ICT is having an effect on society.

One huge potential area for ICT to improve life in our society is in healthcare. The UK Government's Connecting for Health programme aims to make better use of ICT to improve the nation's health. The programmes involve making more effective use of research, moving to electronic rather than paper-based prescriptions and setting up a centralised system for patient records so that they can be accessed at any time by any healthcare professional.

End of sub-topic questions

1 Look at the NHS Connecting for Health website (www. connectingforhealth.nhs.uk/). Write a newspaper article about one of the developments described on the site.

2 Think about the Internet in terms of ethics and morals. What do you think are the big issues that apply to Internet use?

3 Would you prefer the Internet to be more closely regulated? Justify your opinion.

16.2 Consequences of the use of ICT

Consequences of the use of ICT for individuals

The growth in personal computers has had a profound effect on individuals. This has been especially true as the World Wide Web has grown and evolved and it is now the case that a large majority of the population have some form of access to computers. Many people are now sitting in front of a computer for many hours without any real social interaction. The falling price of computers has a lot to do with this growth of use.

Social networking sites such as MySpace and Facebook have never been more popular and many people believe they are an extension to social interaction and not a complete substitute. It has been estimated that as much as 25 per cent of Internet capacity is now used for social networking. Many employers have banned these sites because of their

Fig. 16.4 *New-style call centre*

potential to waste both time and company resources. One telephone enquiry company discovered that 40 per cent of their networking capacity was being used in this way. It is also true that people should perhaps think a little more about the way they portray themselves on these sites. Potential employers may look to see what kind of person they are actually taking on. Two young tennis players lost their funding because they were not deemed to be behaving like professionals judging by what their blogs said they got up to.

Changing employment

As always in an area of rapid change, employment types and prospects will change for individuals. It has always been argued that computers replace individuals and there is no doubt that some traditional jobs have disappeared, like the vast typing pools seen in offices before the large uptake in word processing. However, changes in the use of ICT have enabled new jobs to be created and one of the largest growth areas is through call centres which can only be run using modern ICT systems. The systems for these centres need to be managed and maintained by ICT professionals such as network managers, ICT support staff and maintenance technicians.

The just-in-time approach to large-scale construction projects is another example of how ICT is changing the jobs that people do. Project managers have to use a variety of ICT methods to ensure that materials are delivered on site only as they are ready to be used, and the logistics involved means that it is difficult to work in project management without a significant level of ICT skills.

What other jobs have been replaced or changed by ICT systems? Have they replaced all of the employees or is it the case that employees are reskilled for different jobs that have now been created?

Case study

ICT at British Airways

British Airways chief information officer (CIO) Paul Coby has spoken about ICT systems in use and the changing nature of their costs.

'IT must be available globally, 24/7, and each year we must do more for less,' he told *Computing*.

'We have taken 45 per cent out of the cost of running IT, while what IT does in terms of processing has gone up by a multiple of seven.'

Despite cutting IT staff numbers by half over the past five years, Coby is adding to the department's skillset, and the airline's IT Professional Programme is part of the recruitment drive.

'We have 900 applications for 10 people to work in Heathrow and 10 in Newcastle joining us at an entry level. It is vital to gain stimulus as we must grow our skills as technology moves forward and the business changes', he said.

'There is no room for complacency. We are only as good as today's performance. Our competitors are exceptionally good, and we must keep moving.'

(*Source*: extracted from *Computing* magazine)

The extract shows that cost control is at the forefront of big business operations. Technology costs are being carefully controlled and the emphasis as far as staff are concerned is on smaller numbers with increased levels of skill.

Activity

Fast, accessible, instant communication

What are the key words used in advertisements and literature to proclaim the benefits of ICT systems now and in the future?

How much use does your school/college/library make of ICT? Do some research with your colleagues to find out how much use they make of ICT for their study and revision in comparison to other methods.

Discuss whether you think this has changed over the past five years and if it has, why you think that the changes have occurred.

Changing face of computer use in society

There are very few areas of modern life where computers are not playing an ever-increasing role. Every day you will use many computer-based systems and you can be sure that organisations such as schools, colleges, online retailers and providers of digital TV will be using highly sophisticated ICT systems. As you use the Internet phone that you have just bought, log on to your computer to use a messaging service or listen to your music on the move, take some time to think about the ICT system itself and look beyond the product that has become an integral part of your daily life.

E-learning

It may be that you have already come across some form of e-learning in your school or college. Are you a able to do some form of study or revision online via an intranet system set up by one of your subject departments? Other individuals who are unable to attend the traditional educational setting may be studying for qualifications almost entirely based around using the Internet for their learning. Some educational establishments now allow students to send work in electronically and have it assessed online, saving resources at the same time. This technology can be useful for students in remote areas or those who are not well enough to attend a traditional school.

E-government

A new concept that is becoming popular is e-government, which has many different facets – from the use of ICT to determine policies, online voting and of course government legislation used to protect ICT systems and their users.

Government bodies obviously use ICT in their daily business. Recently, however, the idea of voting online has become a major issue in the use of ICT systems. This idea has become popular and has been trialled in some areas of the UK with mixed success. The government is keen to introduce it further, however, as they see it as a way of increasing the

Activity

Do some research on the concept of e-learning and make a list of some of the educational organisations that are offering online courses. What sort of subjects are they offering?

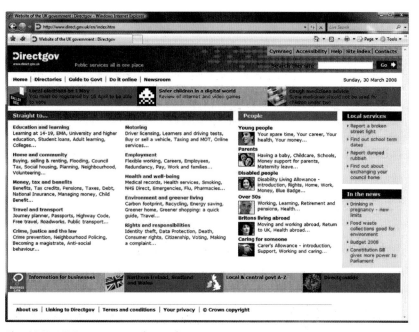

Fig. 16.5 *UK Government web portal*

involvement of the electorate, especially the younger more computer-literate voters who they find difficult to encourage to get involved in politics through the traditional voting system. One use of ICT that has proved popular is for people who have concerns about political issues to be able to set up web-based polls where interested people can post their views.

The government is gradually developing a web portal site, www.direct.gov.uk, which provides links to the many online services that allow citizens of the UK to tax their car, pay their taxes or buy a fishing licence. Many of these services are convenient for the user and represent considerable cost savings compared to traditional methods of tax collection for the government.

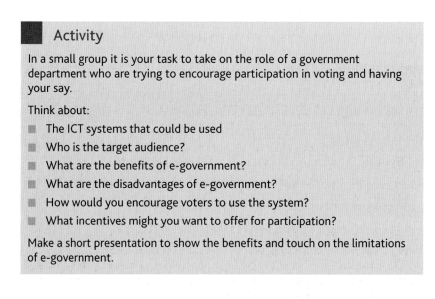

Activity

In a small group it is your task to take on the role of a government department who are trying to encourage participation in voting and having your say.

Think about:

■ The ICT systems that could be used

■ Who is the target audience?

■ What are the benefits of e-government?

■ What are the disadvantages of e-government?

■ How would you encourage voters to use the system?

■ What incentives might you want to offer for participation?

Make a short presentation to show the benefits and touch on the limitations of e-government.

E-commerce

One of the largest areas of growth for traditional commerce and for new entrants to the market is in the area of e-commerce. It is unlikely that any major player in the commercial market does not have an online presence to either add to their high-street activity or, like some companies, such as the bookseller Amazon, trade entirely via the Internet using large warehouse space to store goods which are shipped out when orders are placed by the customers. Access to new innovations has become important and as new technology like e-ticketing is introduced businesses then have to think about the next technology that will keep them ahead of their competitors in terms of ICT systems.

British Airways, for instance, are always looking to innovate and are currently ensuring that they keep up to date with any changes being introduced on the World Wide Web. They make changes to their website monthly to ensure that it works efficiently, and changes to the structure of the site are always being looked into.

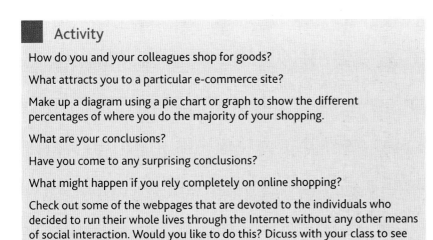

Fig. 16.6 *Online retailers use different secure payment methods*

Activity

How do you and your colleagues shop for goods?

What attracts you to a particular e-commerce site?

Make up a diagram using a pie chart or graph to show the different percentages of where you do the majority of your shopping.

What are your conclusions?

Have you come to any surprising conclusions?

What might happen if you rely completely on online shopping?

Check out some of the webpages that are devoted to the individuals who decided to run their whole lives through the Internet without any other means of social interaction. Would you like to do this? Dicuss with your class to see who might like this kind of lifestyle.

Access to information

Access to vast amounts of data and information is obviously one of the key reasons that ICT systems are used on a daily basis in many organisations. The availability and speed of access can, in general terms, make the daily running of many organisations efficient and cost effective. Passenger information is increasingly available via networked computers, which includes train timetables, information in stations and airports and real-time information over the Internet. This allows for up-to-date information to be available to the public almost instantly via laptop, PDA and, increasingly, new types of mobile technology.

Activity

These are some of the innovations that are being introduced:
- Flight tickets are being sent to customers' mobile phones as a bar code which is stored on the phone and is scanned before check in.
- Biometric fingerprints are being trialled as part of airport security.
- Computer Aid has sent computers to Uganda where weather data is input then processed and information is given directly to farmers to aid decision making.

Do some research into other organisations that use ICT systems extensively and see whether they are trying similar ideas or if they have newer ideas that have not been thought of. The very nature of ICT systems means by the time you are reading this text book, new ideas for the use of ICT systems will be being used, so you must try to continually update your knowledge, including the idea that social, ethical and environmental initiatives need to be considered.

Websites like the following ones are a good source of up-to-date ICT news:

www.computing.co.uk/news/

www.guardian.co.uk/technology

http://news.zdnet.co.uk/

Did you know?

It is possible to set up RSS feeds to deliver technology news to your desktop so that you are always in touch with new developments.

Consequences of the use of ICT for society

With the increasing usage of computers in society comes an increasing risk of over-dependence on them, believing that computers will work in an efficient manner and that nothing will go wrong with them. In reality of course that is not always the case. The first risk is the fact that there may be some kind of failure within the program itself, causing the program to run in an inefficient manner or not at all. There are possibilities of hardware failure, and the consequences of global communication systems failing would be catastrophic.

✔ *In this section you have covered:*

- factors that influence the use of ICT systems
- changes that the use of ICT have had on our culture
- economic consequences of rapidly changing ICT systems
- effects that the use of ICT has on the environment
- ethical and legal considerations that need to be considered when using ICT
- how jobs have changed through the increasing use of ICT
- new ways of using ICT for commerce, government and information gathering
- consequences of the use of ICT systems for individuals and society.

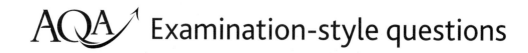
Section 9: ICT systems and their components

1   The figure shows a weekly payslip which has been produced as the output from data that has been input and processed.

(a)   State one item of data that is input each week.   *(1 mark)*

(b)   State two items of data that would be held on the payroll file.   *(2 marks)*

(c)   Explain one process that has taken place in order to produce this payslip.   *(3 marks)*

AQA, 2007

Employee Name				
Joe Jones				

Employee Number	N.I. Number	Tax Code	Tax Period	Date
Z001	ZX212345N	567P	29	22/11/2006

Item Code	Description	Rate	Hours	Amount
01	Basic-Weekly	10.00	46.00	460.00
06	Travel	10.00	7.00	70.00
10	Accommodation			80.00
			TOTAL GROSS PAY	610.00

2   Explain what is meant by the term Information and Communications Technology.   *(3 marks)*

AQA, 2003

3   When Mrs Brown received her gas bill she found that it was for £10,000, which she knew was not correct. When she telephoned the gas company to complain, the explanation she received was that the computer had got it wrong. Describe a more likely explanation.   *(3 marks)*

AQA, 2005

4   Three stages of a data processing system are input, processing and output. State, using an example for each one, what is meant by:

(a)   input   *(2 marks)*

(b)   processing   *(2 marks)*

(c)   output.   *(2 marks)*

AQA, 2005

5   Every ICT task involves the input of data, which is then processed and information is output. Using an example of an ICT task with which you are familiar:

(a)   State what the task is.   *(1 mark)*

(b)   Give one example of data that is input, stating how it is input.   *(2 marks)*

(c)   Describe one process needed to fulfil the task.   *(2 marks)*

(d)   Give one example of information output, stating how it is output.   *(2 marks)*

AQA, 2004

6   People are one of the key components of an ICT system. Name three
other components.   *(3 marks)*

Section 10: Data and information

1   Information is a commodity and it can have a monetary value. State three
factors that could affect the value of information.   *(3 marks)*

AQA, 2006

2   Three stages of a data processing system are input, processing and output.
State, using an example for each one, what is meant by:

(a)   input   *(2 marks)*

(b)   processing   *(2 marks)*

(c)   output.   *(2 marks)*

AQA, 2005

3   Explain, using examples, the following terms as they are applied within ICT:

(a)   data   *(2 marks)*

(b)   information.   *(2 marks)*

AQA, 2005

4   One of the things ICT can provide is a vast storage capacity.

(a)   How is this of benefit to an organisation?   *(1 mark)*

(b)   Give two other things that ICT can provide and, for each one,
state a different benefit.   *(4 marks)*

5   The quality of information is important and if information is inaccurate it
loses value. Describe two other factors that will determine the quality and
value of information.   *(4 marks)*

Section 11: People and ICT systems

1   ICT professionals require certain personal qualities to enable them to do
their job well. Describe three personal qualities that they should have.   *(6 marks)*

AQA, 2007

2   For the successful introduction of a new or updated information system,
an organisation needs to have clear management objectives
and effective staff teams.

(a)   Describe two characteristics of an effective ICT team.   *(4 marks)*

AQA, 2004

3   You have been asked to write a job description for a vacancy on a
software company's help-desk team. State, giving a reason for each one,
two personal qualities that are relevant to the job, which you would ask
for in the description.   *(4 marks)*

AQA, 2003

4   Describe the characteristics of a natural language interface. Illustrate
your answer with two different examples of use of this type of interface.   *(4 marks)*

AQA, 2005

5 A common human/computer interface is a graphical user interface (GUI). State three features of a GUI and, for each one, describe how it provides an effective method of communication between the user and a computer system.

(6 marks)

AQA, 2006

6 Many retailers are expanding their e-commerce operations.

(a) Identify one current job for which ICT professionals are being recruited within e-commerce.

(1 mark)

(b) All ICT professionals require certain personal characteristics in order to work effectively. Using the job you have suggested in (a), give two personal characteristics for the ICT professional to work effectively, and explain why you consider these characteristics would be essential.

(4 marks)

(c) Discuss the benefits and limitations of using websites shopping to retailers and their customers.

(9 marks)

(d) Explain two factors that you think should be considered when designing a web interface for use by customers that would support good customer management.

(4 marks)

7 Explain two factors that you think should be considered when designing a user interface for an end user of an ICT system that would help with their interaction with the system.

(4 marks)

Section 12: Transfer of data in ICT systems

1 Describe two possible differences between a LAN and a WAN.

(4 marks)

AQA, 2005

2 A company is having a 16-station LAN installed.

(a) Describe what is meant by the term 'local area network'.

(2 marks)

(b) State three items of hardware and/or software that could be needed if the LAN is to be connected to the Internet.

(3 marks)

AQA, 2007

3 There are 10 employees in a local estate agent's office. Each employee uses a networked PC on a LAN.

(a) Give four benefits to the office of using a network rather than stand-alone PCs.

(4 marks)

(b) The office is part of a national chain that is connected together over a WAN. Explain the difference between a LAN and a WAN.

(4 marks)

(c) Give two benefits to the estate agent's office of using the WAN.

(2 marks)

(d) The local office has purchased a digital camera to take pictures of the houses that it is selling. Give two benefits to the office of using a digital camera.

(2 marks)

4 (a) Explain what is meant by the terms Internet and World Wide Web.

(4 marks)

(b) Give one reason why a de facto standard might become popular in the ICT industry.

(1 mark)

(c) Discuss the benefits of a de jure standard being implemented in the ICT industry.

(2 marks)

Section 13: Safety and security of ICT systems

1 An employee illegally copies a piece of software and takes it home. The employee has committed a crime.

   (a) Give two other examples of crime involving the use of ICT. *(2 marks)*

   (b) Malpractice:

   (i) Explain what is meant by malpractice in relation to ICT. *(2 marks)*

   (ii) Give two ICT examples of malpractice. *(2 marks)*

   AQA, 2006

2 (a) Name the following:

   (i) legislation designed to protect companies and individuals who produce software; *(1 mark)*

   (ii) legislation designed to protect the privacy of individuals whose personal data is held by others. *(1 mark)*

   (b) State two duties of the Information Commissioner. *(2 marks)*

   AQA, 2006

3 Information systems need to be protected from both internal and external threats.

   (a) Explain, using examples, the differences between an internal and an external threat to an information system. *(4 marks)*

   (b) Describe one measure that a company can take to protect its information system from:

   (i) internal threats; *(2 marks)*

   (ii) external threats. *(2 marks)*

   AQA, 2005

4 ICT systems have to be protected from both malpractice and crime. Using an example for each one, explain what is meant by:

   (a) malpractice; *(3 marks)*

   (b) crime. *(3 marks)*

   AQA, 2005

5 ICT systems are vulnerable to different threats such as a natural disaster.

   (a) State one other threat to an ICT system. *(1 marks)*

   (b) Discuss some of the measures that an organisation might use to protect their ICT systems from internal and external threats. *(6 marks)*

Section 14: Procedures for backup and recovery

1 A student is working on an ICT project using the computers at her school and her own computer at home. Describe a suitable backup procedure that the student could use. *(4 marks)*

   AQA, 2004

2 List four topics that should be included in an organisation's backup strategy. *(4 marks)*

   AQA, 2007

3 A company is reviewing its backup and recovery procedures.

   (a) Describe three items that should be included in a backup procedure. *(6 marks)*

(b)   State three actions that should be part of a recovery procedure.

(3 marks)

AQA, 2006

4   Discuss the relative benefits and limitations of the different forms of backup that are available to an organisation. You should include the procedures used and the different hardware and software that is required in each of the different methods. In this question you will be marked on your ability to use good English, to organise information clearly and to use specialist vocabulary where appropriate.

(14 marks)

Section 15: Use of ICT systems

1   Name two types of processing that can be used with a computer system.

(2 marks)

AQA, 2004

2   (a)   Explain, using a suitable example, what the term 'batch processing' means.

(3 marks)

    (b)   Explain, using a suitable example, what the term 'transaction processing' means.

(3 marks)

AQA, 2005

3   A theatre booking system uses interactive transaction processing. Explain what is meant by the terms 'interactive processing' and 'transaction processing'.

(4 marks)

AQA, 2006

4   Name a mode of processing that would be suitable for each of the following ICT systems:

    (a)   airline ticket-booking system *(1 mark)*

    (b)   production of electricity bills *(1 mark)*

    (c)   Internet banking *(1 mark)*

Section 16: Factors and consequences of ICT

1   A school wishes to allow its students access to the Internet for their course work. However the head teacher is concerned that unrestricted access to the Internet might cause some problems. State four problems about which the head teacher might be concerned and for each one explain a measure that could be taken to try to prevent the problem.

(8 marks)

AQA, 2007

2   For each of the following organisations, state one use it can make of ICT and give one benefit to the organisation of this use; the uses of ICT must be different in each case:

    (a)   a newspaper *(2 marks)*

    (b)   a supermarket *(2 marks)*

    (c)   a travel company *(2 marks)*

    (d)   the Police. *(2 marks)*

AQA, 2006

3   Discuss two of the factors that might influence the use of an ICT system in an organisation.

(4 marks)

4   Discuss the benefits and limitations of the use of ICT systems for individuals and society.

(6 marks)

Index

A

access rights   60, 136
algorithm   134
ALU (Arithmetic and Logic
   Unit)   98
analysis   56
   identifying input, processing and
      output   61–2
   identifying problems   56
   identifying requirements   56–8,
      61
   requirements
      specifications   58–61
animation software   40, 47
anti-virus software   139
applications software   33
   choosing   45–7
   moving images   39–40
   multimedia   42–4
   numbers   37–8
   pictures   38–9
   sound   40–2
   text   33–7
archive storage   29–30
Arithmetic and Logic Unit
   (ALU)   98
audience   56, 78, 97

B

back pain and computer use   50
backing storage   25
backup   142–52
   and continuity of
      service   148–50
   responsibilities for   149–50
   storage location   150
   storage media   30, 147–8
   strategies   143–47
bar-codes   10, 106
batch processing   159
binary numbers   104
BIOS   25
bitmap software   38–9, 46
bits   102
Bluetooth   11, 13, 20
boundary data   74
bytes   104

C

cameras   11–12, 39
card readers   8
CDs   27, 29, 147
Central Processing Unit (CPU)   98

changes, tracking   35
check digits   64
client-server networks   123–4
clients   56, 97
   approval of system design   69
   requirements   57–8, 61, 77
   training for   69
codes of practice   98
coding (of data)   102–4
command-line
   interfaces   113–4,116
commerce, ICT and   171
Computer Misuse Act 1990   137–8
computer networking   120
   advantages of   120–1
   characteristics of
      networks   121–5
   Internet and WWW   126–7
   printers and   23–4
   security software   135
   standards   127–8
computer outage   149
concept keyboards   5
Control Unit   98
Copyright, Designs and Patents Act
   1988   139–40
CPU (Central Processing
   Unit)   98
crime   131
criteria   36
cross field checks   64
CRT monitors   16
culture and ICT   162

D

DAT tapes   27, 30
data   97–8, 101–6
   analysis software   46
   backup and recovery   142–52
   coding and encoding   102–4
   input design   63–6, 85–6
   input devices   4–14
   processing   105, 153, 159–60
   processing design   66–8, 76, 86
   protection   129–41
   searching   153–4
   storage   25–30, 153
   test   74
   transfer   123–5
   types   102
data capture forms   9–10, 13, 64–5
Data Protection Act 1998   136–7
database management
   systems   35–7, 46, 66–7

de facto standards   127
de jure standards   127
default values   84
design, system   56, 108
   analysis of problem   56–62
   appropriateness of solutions   158
   client approval   69
   evaluation   81–8
   implementation planning   71–3
   implementation process   73
   input design   63–6
   output design   68–9
   processing design   66–8
   testing   69, 74–80
   tools and techniques
      selection   62
   training for clients and end-
      users   69
   see also ICT systems
desktop publishing (DTP)   35, 46
differential backup   145, 147
digital cameras   11–12, 39
digital homes   124–5
digital projectors   16
digitising tablets   6–7
disabilities, people with
   input devices for   12
   output devices for   20–1
disaster recovery planning
   (DRP)   149–51
Display Screens Equipment
   Regulations   49–50
dot-matrix printers   17–18
DTP (desktop publishing)   35, 46
DVDs   27, 29, 147

E

e-commerce   171
e-government   169–70
e-learning   169
e-mail software   43–4
economic factors and ICT   163–4
efficient solutions   84
EFTPOS   163
electronic point of sale (EPOS)   10
employees and system
   security   131, 135–6
employment
   ICT and   168–9
   working in ICT   116–19
encoding (of data)   102–4
encryption of data   133–4
end-users   56, 99
   characteristics of   108–11

interaction with
   systems **111–15**
  requirements **56–8, 78**
  training for **69**
entity 36
environmental factors and
  ICT **164**
ergonomics 50
erroneous data 74
error messages 63
ethics and ICT **165–6**
expert systems **95**
extranets **121**
eye strain and computer use **53**

F

fields 35, 36
file compression 25
files, transferring **29**
firewalls 139–40
flash memory **27–8, 29, 30**
flat file database 35
floppy disks **26, 30**
format checks **63**
forms **9–10, 13, 35, 36, 64–5**
full backup **144–5, 147**

G

games controllers **12–13**
Gantt chart 71
government, ICT and **169–70**
**graphical user interface
(GUI) 111–12, 116**
graphics software **38–9, 46–7**
graphics tablets **6–7, 16**

H

hard disks **25, 26, 28–9**
  and backup **31, 147**
hardware **98–9**
  input devices **4–14**
  output devices **15–24**
  protection measures **134–5**
  storage devices **25–30, 147–8**
headaches and computer use **53**
headphones **20**
health and safety
  of ICT systems **49–53**
  of software **53–4**
Health and Safety at Work Act
  1974 **49**
healthcare, ICT and **167**
homes, digital **124–5**
hot swap 26
house style 59
**HTML (Hypertext Markup
Language) 43, 127, 128**
HTTP (HyperText Transfer
  Protocol) **127, 128**
hubs 121–2

I

ICT 94
  working in **116–19**
ICT systems **95–8**
  advantages **153–7**
  appropriateness **157**
  backup and recovery **142–52**
  components of **97–100**
  consequences of use **167–72**
  factors influencing use **162–7**
  health and safety **49–53**
  networks **120–28**
  processing types **159–61**
  safety and security **129–40**
  software **32–3**
  users and **108–16**
  see also design, system
**IDU (Instruction Decoding
Unit) 98**
images *see* moving images;
  photographs; pictures
incremental backup **145–6, 147**
information **99, 101, 105**
  access to **155–6, 172**
  limitations on information
    produced **158**
  output design **68–9, 76–7, 86**
  output devices **15–24**
  presentation **154**
  quality of **105–6**
inkjet printers **17, 23**
input **94**
  design of data entry **63–6,
    85–6**
  identifying **61–2**
input devices **4–13, 63**
  choosing **13–14**
**input, process and output
(IPO) 94**
**Instruction Decoding Unit
(IDU) 98**
interactive 42
interactive processing **159–60**
interactive whiteboards **6, 16, 47**
interfaces *see* **user interfaces**
Internet 126–7, 165
Internet Protocol (IP) 128
interviews, to identify
  requirements **56–7**
intranets **121**
intuitive solutions 85
ISBN **104**

J

job design **50**

K

keyboards **4, 5, 51–2**
keypads **4**

knowledge-based systems **95**

L

laser printers **17, 22–3**
layout tools **34**
learning, ICT and **169**
legislation
  health and safety **49–50**
  and ICT systems **98, 136–40**
length checks **64**
list/lookup checks **64, 75**
**local area network (LAN) 120,
122, 125**

M

**magnetic ink character recognition
(MICR) 10**
magnetic storage **25–7, 147**
malpractice 131
menu-driven interfaces **112–13,
116**
**metropolitan area network
(MAN) 120**
mirrored drives 26
mobile phone screens **16–17**
monitors **15–17, 21–2, 49–50**
mouse **5, 52–3**
moving images **11, 39–40**
multi-function printers **17**
multimedia 42–4, 47
multipart stationery 17–18
music **10–11, 41–2**

N

network switches 123
networks **120–5**
  advantages of **120–1**
  characteristics of **121–5**
  Internet and WWW **126–7**
  printers and **23–4**
  security software **135**
  standards **127–8**
normal data 74
numbers, software for **37–8**

O

observation, and problem
  analysis **58**
operating system **32–3**
**optical character recognition
(OCR) 9–10**
**optical mark recognition
(OMR) 9**
optical storage devices **27, 29, 30,
147–8**
output **15, 96, 99**
  design **61–2, 68–9, 76–7,
86**
output devices **15–21**
  choosing **21–4**

P

PDAs **6, 17, 21**
peer-to-peer networks **121–3**
people, as component of ICT
 systems **97**
photographs
 digital cameras **11–12**
 printing **19–20**
 software **38–9, 46–7**
pictures
 software for **38–9, 46–7**
 see also moving images;
 photographs
pixels 11, 15, 38
plasma screens **16, 22**
plotters **18**
presence checks **63, 75**
presentations
 design procedures **68**
 software **42–3**
printers **17–18**
 choosing **22–4**
 printing photographs **19**
printing services **19**
problems, analysing **56**
procedures **98, 135–6**
processing **96, 105, 153**
 design of **61–2, 66–8, 76, 86**
 types of **159–61**
projectors, digital **16**
proofing tools **34**
protocols 128
prototyping **73**

Q

queries, database **37**
questionnaires, to identify
 requirements **56–7**

R

radio frequency ID (RFID) 8, 104
RAID drives 26, 30, 123
RAM 25
range checks **63**
Really Simple Syndication (RSS)
 feeds 44
records 35, 36
recovery
 and continuity of service **148–9**
 data storage location **148**
 responsibilities for **148**
relational databases 36–7
removable media 25, 26–7, 29–30
repetitive strain injury (RSI) **50–1**
reports **36**
requirements specifications **58–61,**
 81–2
resolution 15
RFID (radio frequency ID) 8, 104

risk assessments **49, 144**
robust solutions 86
ROM 25
routers 122–3
RSI (repetitive strain injury) **50–1**
RSS (Really Simple Syndication)
 feeds 44

S

safety *see* health and safety; security
sample rates 10, 40
sampling 10
scanners **8–9, 39**
screens **15–17, 21–2**
 health and safety **49–50**
 touch **6, 7, 16, 53, 113**
search facilities **153–4**
Secure Socket Layer (SSL) **133**
security
 legislation **136–40**
 need to protect data **129–30**
 protecting ICT systems **134–6**
 threats to ICT systems **131–4**
security attacks 135
security mechanisms 139
security services 139
servers **123, 148**
skills, ICT **97, 114–15, 117–19**
social factors and ICT **166–7**
social networking **167–8**
software **32, 98**
 applications software **33–44**
 choosing applications
 software **45–7**
 health and safety of **53–4**
 and security **129, 135, 139**
 systems software **32–3**
solutions *see* design, system
sorts, database **36**
sound **10, 40–2, 47**
speakers **20**
speech recognition **7**
spinal damage and computer
 use **50**
spreadsheets **37–8, 46, 66**
spyware **132**
SSL (Secure Socket Layer) **133**
standards **127–128**
storage of data
 and backup **30, 146–7, 149**
 choosing storage devices **28–30**
 file compression **25**
 reasons for **25**
 types of storage **25–8**
 vast capacity of ICT
 systems **153**
stress and computer-based
 work **54**
styles **34**
stylus 6

sub-tasks **71**
system design *see* design, system
systems **94**
 see also ICT systems
systems software **32–3**

T

TCP (Transmission Control
 Protocol) 128
teamwork **118**
teleworking **166**
templates **34**
test plans and planning **69,**
 74–80
text, software for **33–7, 46**
TFT monitors **16, 21**
time plans **71–3**
touch screens **6, 7, 53, 113**
trackballs **5**
trackpads **5**
trackpoints **5**
training
 for clients and end-users **69**
 health and safety **50**
transaction processing **160–1**
transcription errors 75
Transmission Control
 Protocol(TCP) 128

U

user interfaces 59, 108–19
 command line **113–14, 116**
 designing **53–4, 65–6, 68, 76,**
 111–13
 graphical **112–13, 116**
 menu-driven **112–13, 116**
user names and passwords 138
users *see* **end-users**
utility software **33**

V

validation 36, 63–4, 75–6
value judgement 57
VDUs (visual display units) **15–16,**
 21, 49–50
vector graphics 39, 46
verification 64
video
 editing software **39–40**
 input **11–12**
video conferencing 11
virus checkers 139
viruses 131, 133,

W

web browsers **44**
web design
 and output devices **22**
 procedures **68**
 software **43, 47**

webcams **12**
whiteboards, interactive **6, 16, 47**
wide area network (WAN) **120**
Wii **13**

wireless networks **121–5**
wizards **34, 36**
word processing software **34–5, 46**
workgroup printers **23**

workstation design **50**
World Wide Web (WWW) **127, 167**
worms **133**